ORCHIDS

dearest Neddy,

Happy Christmas, my own darling,

love
your
Stephanie
'90

ORCHIDS

Their Care and Cultivation

DAVID LEIGH

CASSELL

Cassell Publishers Limited
Artillery House, Artillery Row
London SW1P 1RT

First published 1990

British Library Cataloguing in Publication Data

Leigh, David
Orchids.
1. Orchids. Cultivation
I. Title
635.9'3415

ISBN 0-304-31968-6

Produced by Justin Knowles Publishing Group
9 Colleton Crescent, Exeter EX2 4BY

Editor: Roy Gasson

Typeset by Keyspools Ltd
Printed and bound in Hong Kong

CONTENTS

ACKNOWLEDGEMENTS

Firstly my thanks to my neighbour Keith Andrew, whose orchids feature prominently among the photographs, and to Brian and Wilma Rittershausen, and of course Peter and Arthur, at Burnham Nurseries, for their help and warm welcome during my several photographic visits. Also, and in random order, I would like to thank: Ray Bilton at McBean's Orchids, David at David Stead Orchids, Allan Long at Mansell and Hatcher, Eddie and Gill at Wyld Court Orchids, Bob and Paddy Dadd at Greenaway Orchids, and a good friend, John Gay. Thanks also to Paul and Mary Phillips at Ratcliffes Orchids, and to Terry Adnams at Thatched Lodge Orchids, who also extended kind invitations to visit their nurseries.

Plush, Dorset, 1989

LIST OF PLATES

INTRODUCTION

No other flowers have attracted so many myths and legends as have orchids, some true or at least based on truth, and many quite ridiculous. Men have abandoned their homes to scour the jungles of the world, enduring the most appalling hardships, to find them. Fortunes have been made from them and fortunes have been spent on them. Apparently sane and honourable men have cheated and lied to acquire them. They still retain a fascination unique among flowers and exert an uncanny power over those who fall under their spell.

Why should this be? We know that flowers cannot be sinister or evil. We know (I hope) that none eat any living creatures, let alone us, and yet when fiction creates a dangerous plant it is often an orchid. Is there any reason for this bad press?

A suggestion. Hardly a theory or even a hypothesis, but merely an idle thought. Flowers are aesthetically beautiful and serene products of nature, at least to us, because they exude the calm of radial symmetry. Ask anyone to draw a flower and they will draw the shape of a daisy – that's what we think of as a flower.

But orchid flowers do not have this kind of symmetry. They have only one plane of symmetry, and that is vertical, so that the left side of the flower is a mirror image of the right. They are, that is to say, zygomorphic. Now animals, all animals including us, have this one plane of symmetry – we see it reversed when we look in a mirror. Is it this that makes orchid flowers seem different, somehow not quite right? Is it because we associate this kind of symmetry with animals, not plants at all, and that the association is in some strange and unexplained way disturbing?

I cannot hope, in this book, to look comprehensively at the family. What I might hope is to give some flavour, in text and pictures, of the diversity and fascination of orchids. But be warned, orchiditis is both highly infectious and contagious – it can even be caught from the pages of a book. It is, fortunately, never fatal, but evidence suggests that it is incurable. It strikes everywhere and anywhere – there are pockets of infection throughout the world, known as orchid societies, where a welcome is always available to a fellow sufferer. It strikes anyone, even the wary and the forewarned. It infects rich and poor alike. Emperors and kings have caught it. Statesmen, politicians, and the generally famous suffer. It even attacks the intelligent – Charles Darwin had a serious bout of it. I have had it for many years.

If you catch it, then welcome from a fellow sufferer. Once hooked you will never return to fuchsias and geraniums, and the tomatoes and chrysanthemums in the greenhouse will never seem interesting again.

I

THE ORCHID FAMILY

The orchid family, Orchidaceae, is probably the largest family of flowering plants. Authorities vary with their estimates, but there are between 15,000 and 30,000 species, classified into 750 or so genera. There may be many more – we cannot be exact because new discoveries are made all the time, in many parts of the world, and because new evidence and information leads to revisions by the botanists, some tending to group similar orchids as variations of a single species and thereby giving rise to lower estimates, and others preferring to describe these variations as separate species. The number of new discoveries, particularly in the tropics, should not be underestimated, and it is not always small and insignificant species that come to light. Several spectacular new species have quite recently been introduced from western China, and there can be no doubt that there will be many more to follow from this little-explored area, and from other areas around the world.

What then are the characteristics that make a plant an orchid? Within such a large family we would be right to expect enormous variation in form, but there are some common features.

1. The male and female parts of the flower, the pistil and the stamen, are at least partly and, in all but a few, completely united into one structure, the column.
2. Orchids have very many very small seeds.
3. One of the three petals is modified; it differs from the other two. Because this petal is opposite to the column, the flower is zygomorphic.

4. Most orchid flowers are resupinate (the bud twists through 180° during development, so the flower opens inverted).
5. Orchid pollen, rather than being loose and powdery, is bound together in a few large masses, called pollinia.

Other plants display some of these features – begonias, for example, have very small and numerous seeds – but it is only within the orchids that we find them all, and there are other characteristics of orchids that are almost, but not quite, universal. These though are the main features that make orchid flowers different from other flowers.

Orchids grow everywhere – well, almost everywhere that plants can survive on land (there are no true aquatics). There are no orchids in Antarctica, nor in the far north of the Arctic, although there are representatives almost to the limit of vegetation. There are none at the tops of the highest mountains nor in the most arid deserts. Every other geographic and climatic region has its orchid flora, although it is fair to say that they are by no means evenly distributed, either geographically or ecologically.

The orchids appear to have evolved relatively recently among plant families, and to be still in a state of active evolution. Current thinking suggests that the first primitive orchids probably evolved from a lily-like ancestor during the second quarter of the Cretaceous period, approximately 120 to 100 million years ago. At that time the earth's climate was considerably warmer than it is today, tropical forests covered much of the land, and there were no ice caps. The land masses of the world were still joined in one large continent, Gondwanaland, centred around the present continent of Africa. The primitive ancestors of all the different tribes of orchids had thus already evolved before the continents had divided off and drifted apart into much the shapes and positions we know today. Some types of orchids, which had completed most of their evolution before the drift began, were separated as the continents grew apart, so we find some quite similar orchids growing on different continents. These are the orchids that we see as more or less primitive types. Other, more advanced types, that evolved after the separation of the continents, remain confined to one land mass, in aggregations of similar genera.

Orchids, by evolving a most ingenious range of different life styles, have adapted to a wider range of habitats than have most plants.

Terrestrials

Most plants grow in the ground, deriving their nutrients for growth from the soil via their roots. About one in four of all orchids live in this conventional way, mostly in the more temperate areas of the globe. Native European orchids all belong to this group, as do most orchids of North America, northern Asia, and Australia. Most of these orchids are deciduous and most develop tubers to carry them through the harsher part of the year. In warmer areas growth is confined to the damper and milder winter period, followed by flowering in the spring. In colder regions the growth period is spring, followed by flowering in summer.

There are some terrestrial orchids in the tropics, notably the popular slipper orchids of southeast Asia, but it is as members of the next group that orchids excel in these warmer and wetter climates.

Epiphytes

Epiphytes are plants that grow on other plants, usually trees or bushes, and about three in four of all orchids grow in this way. Epiphytes do not directly derive any nourishment from the host, and should not be confused with parasites, such as mistletoe, which do.

Of all plant species perhaps 30,000 or so have taken to the trees, with more than half of these being orchids. But why should they have evolved this apparently precarious way of life?

Tropical forests are rightly thought of as very rich and diverse ecosystems, but the nutrients are bound up in the luxuriant plant growth, and the soil is often very poor. The recycling of these nutrients back into plant growth, through decay after death, is very rapid and thorough in these climates, leaving little reservoir of nutrients in the soil. So, on the basis of nutrients, life on the ground may not be that much better for the orchids. Then, too, tropical forest floors are dark places where plants have great problems. Forest clearings, created when trees fall, rapidly become temporary islands of lush vegetation, as saplings compete to fill the hole in the canopy. The terrestrial jewel orchids of southeast Asia, with their beautifully marked and variegated foliage, are among the few orchids able to grow in the gloom of the tropical forest floor. So there are drawbacks to life on the ground, whereas the forest canopy offers the great advantages of abundant light and air, together with the presence of pollinators and the lack of terrestrial herbivores. There are also obvious advantages for a family whose seeds are almost exclusively dispersed by wind.

Life off the ground does, however, have its own problems, the most important being a lack of water, or at least a regular supply, and a lack of nutrients. Most tropical climates are not as evenly wet as we may think, but have one, and sometimes two, annual dry seasons. Orchids often bloom during dry spells, when pollinators are more mobile.

Epiphytes have adapted to overcome this difficulty in many ingenious ways. Many orchids have fleshy, and often quite leathery, leaves that help to store water during dry periods. But it is by evolving pseudobulbs that the orchid has met the problem of water storage. The pseudobulb, or false bulb, is a swollen stem extending between two nodes (to produce a bulb shape) or encompassing several nodes (to produce a stem or cane-like structure).

As a consequence of the problems of dehydration, epiphytic orchids are confined to the tropics and sub-tropics, with a few in wet temperate forests, for instance in New Zealand. While there are very many epiphytic orchids in the tropical lowland rain forests (what we traditionally think of as jungle), there are even more to be found in the cooler tropical montane forests, where the changes of temperature, particularly between day and night, create almost constant very high humidity. Very many of our most popular orchids originate in these montane forests, particularly those of South America. Perhaps the most diverse of all epiphytic floras are to be found in the vegetative luxuriance of the cloud forests of the eastern slopes of the Andes.

Orchids are relatively slow-growing plants, and are therefore very tolerant of low substrate fertility. What they do need comes from decaying humus in the nooks and crannies of the bark of the host tree, from air-borne debris that collects around their tangle of roots, and from the droppings of birds and arboreal animals. Orchids have been observed to be particularly numerous on hollow trees used as roosts by bats, presumably because the bats deposit a nitrogen-rich fertilizer throughout the canopy. Some species produce vertical spiky roots to entangle and collect falling leaves and other debris.

There are very many different habitats in a forest, each suitable for epiphytes, and each with its characteristic orchids. Many tall trees adapt to shallow soils by developing large, often buttressed, boles, or prop roots, creating large crevices in which leaf debris collects to form humus. Here we find orchids which may normally be terrestrials, growing in what must be very similar conditions to their more conventional situation. These often large species bridge the gap between epiphytes and terrestrials, and extend farther up the tree, where large branch crotches create a similar refuge. Others, such as *Vanilla*, bridge the gap by starting life on the ground and extending their growth continuously as climbers, eventually abandoning the base of the plant as they take to the trees. Farther up, there are other humus-growing orchids to be found in the forks of smaller branches, and particularly on horizontal branches. Some will find a home on the trunks, clinging to the bark – even the smoothest of barks, which appear to offer little foothold, have their share of species. Farther on and up we find many small species of orchids on ever-smaller branches, with even the smallest of twigs having their characteristic orchid flora.

Orchids appear to be selective in choosing their host tree, with humus growers being the least selective, and the small twig epiphytes being particularly so. Some orchid species are confined to only a few, or even perhaps only one, species of host tree, but this does not seem to persist in cultivation. Presumably extremes of selectivity are related to the process of germination and establishment of young plants. *Cymbidiella rhodochila*, a most beautiful epiphytic orchid from Madagascar usually grows on a particular acacia (*Albitzia fastigiata*), and always in association with an epiphytic staghorn fern (*Platycerium madagascariense*). This orchid has always had the reputation of being rather difficult, and advice on cultivation often recommends that it be grown in a basket with the fern, some authorities maintaining that it will never grow without this association. I have, however, grown it myself from seed to flowering, in pots and with normal orchid compost, without any particular problems.

Lithophytes

Some orchids grow on rocks and cliffs, and are known as lithophytes, or rock dwellers. Most species so described also grow as terrestrials or as epiphytes, or even as both. It is therefore perhaps misleading to think of lithophytes as a separate group at all – they should be considered instead as epiphytes or terrestrials that have taken advantage of an opportunity offered by an outcrop of rock or a cliff face.

Saprophytes

Saprophytes are plants that live on dead and decaying plant material. Because they bypass the process of photosynthesis they have no need of chlorophyll, and are therefore not green, and they can grow successfully in situations where the light would be insufficient for green plants. They have no significant leaves and their root system has been modified for their strange existence. Most saprophytic orchids are found in the tropics as terrestrials or as climbers. Since they are not dependent on light they are often very fast growers, with 6in (15cm) per day reported for some climbers. Of all orchids the saprophytes are the least understood, in part because they are virtually impossible to cultivate, and thereby study, in captivity.

2

THE ORCHID PLANT

Growth Patterns

Orchids are monocotyledons and so they lack the tissue that would allow their stems to continue to increase in diameter: with dicotyledons the cambium becomes woody and mechanically strong and so is able to support a larger and larger plant. Monocotyledons are therefore limited in size and have had to develop other growth strategies. Their two main growth patterns are known as sympodial and monopodial.

Sympodial

Sympodial growth is where one growth is produced – and matures and flowers, usually within one year – from the base of the previous season's growth. With some orchids, for example cattleyas, flowering takes place when the season's growth is mature, often to coincide with a drier period more favourable for pollinators. Others, including the popular deciduous dendrobiums, wait through the dry season and flower just as the next wet growing season is about to commence. A variation adopted by coelogynes and others is to flower at the end of the dry rest from the emerging new season's growth. Flowers may emerge from the growths either laterally (from the leaf axils), as with cymbidiums, dendrobiums, and odontoglossums, or terminally (from the end of the growth) as with cattleyas and coelogynes. Most orchids, and all those that have pseudobulbs, have a sympodial growth pattern.

Monopodial

From sympodial ancestors have evolved the mono-podial (one-foot) orchids. With this exclusively epiphytic group the stem elongates indefinitely in one direction with leaves arranged alternately on either side, and the roots and inflorescences arise laterally from the leaf axils, or from a position immediately opposite them. The leaves may be close together, with the stem very much compressed, as with members of the genus *Phalaenopsis*, or very much separated, to form a vine-like climber such as *Vanilla*. From time to time a side branch will grow from one of the dormant buds found in each leaf axil, and species that are particularly prone to this branching can eventually form large scrambling clumps. As they elongate and branch indefinitely, eventually dying off at the other end, it is often impossible to decide which bit belongs to which individual plant in the tangle of roots and stems.

The majority of monopodials are found in the Old World, with the greatest concentration in southeast Asia. Most, but by no means all, inhabit climatic regions where there is little if any dry season, so the lack of pseudobulbs presents no great problem. As a result they are popular in cultivation, where, in the appropriate conditions, they will reward the grower with blooms at any season, often more than once a year. A well-cultivated phalaenopsis, for instance, can be in flower all year round.

With either growth type the orchid plant is continually progressing either sideways (in sympodials) or upwards (in monopodials), with the older parts of the plant eventually dying and rotting away. The life span of an individual plant is therefore theoretically infinite, being terminated only by outside influences, for example the death of the host tree. Orchids do not die of old age.

A few genera of rather obscure New World orchids have a growth pattern intermediate between monopodial and sympodial, displaying characteristics of both styles. These are known as pseudomonopodials.

Plant Structure

A brief outline of the structure of orchid plants follows, ending with the most interesting parts, flowers.

Rhizomes

Rhizomes, found only in sympodial orchids, are horizontal stems, in or on the growing medium, consisting of the initial basal sections of a succession of annual growths joined together. Each new growth produces first a new section of rhizome and then turns upwards to form a shoot, a cane, or a pseudobulb according to the species. From this point will come next year's growth to form initially a further extension of the rhizome.

The rhizome is often covered with papery bracts, and can vary in thickness and length. A short rhizome gives rise to tufted plants such as masdevallias or many odontoglossums. Cattleyas have strong rhizomes of intermediate length that space out the pseudobulbs. Many coelogynes and bulbophyllums have elongated and wiry rhizomes between well-spaced pseudobulbs, giving the plant a straggly appearance.

Roots

The roots of orchids have evolved many different variations of form, particularly in those orchids that have to cope with the problems of an epiphytic existence. Orchids do not develop a main tap root but produce only secondary roots, which arise from the rhizome in the case of sympodials and from the stem in the case of monopodials. Orchids do not produce the branched, fibrous root systems that we associate with most plants – although some have quite thin and wiry roots orchids generally have relatively thick and little-branched root systems. Despite the considerable lengths to which some, notably the aerial roots of epiphytes, may grow, they do not taper, remaining much the same diameter throughout.

The roots of most orchids consist of a relatively thin and wiry core covered with a spongy layer of dead and hollow cells called the velamen. The velamen is particularly important for epiphytes, because it rapidly absorbs water and nutrients, passing this stored water to the root core over time. The velamen gives most orchid roots their characteristic grey colour, which is lighter when dry. Aerial roots of epiphytes are often flattened on one side where they cling to the bark of the host tree, but they are generally round when they hang in the air. Several members of the genus *Phalaenopsis* produce roots so flattened as to be almost ribbon-like, which cling tenaciously to even very smooth surfaces. The growing tip of an aerial root is green, and its presence and length indicates that the plant is in active growth. Green chlorophyll is present to a greater or lesser extent in the roots of epiphytes, and particularly in the root tips. There are even some epiphytic orchids that have no leaves at all and so rely entirely on their green roots for photosynthesis.

Pseudobulbs

Pseudobulbs are swollen secondary stems. They represent the main way in which sympodial orchids have evolved to survive dry periods, particularly important in the case of epiphytes. They vary considerably in form, shape, and size, often to a surprising extent even within the same genus. Some species of *Bulbophyllum* have pseudobulbs smaller than a match head, while those of the giant *Grammatophyllum speciosum* are as thick as a man's arm and several metres long. Some species in the genus *Schomburgkia*, relatives of the cattleyas, have developed hollow pseudobulbs in which live colonies of ants. The ants benefit from the protection offered by a readymade home and in return offer some protection for the plant from insect pests, although these orchids can thrive perfectly well in cultivation without their live-in caretakers.

Leaves

The leaves of orchids are arranged on either side of the stem, alternately left and right, at each node. They are generally strap-shaped, tongue-shaped, or

ORCHIDS

oval-elliptical, with often pronounced and typically monocotyledonous parallel veins. The leaves of cattleyas and many others are very tough and leathery, to withstand quite harsh conditions, and persist on the plant for several years, whereas those of many deciduous species of *Lycaste* are quite thin and delicate and are easily burned in strong sunlight.

There are a few orchids with exceptional leaves and some with no leaves at all. The jewel orchids (*Haemaria*, *Anoectochilus*, and *Macodes*) have green or deep purple-brown leaves delicately net-veined with silver, gold, or red. Many of the species of slipper orchids (*Paphiopedilum*) have leaves tessellated in two shades of green. The European common spotted orchid (*Dactylorhiza fuchsii*) has spotted leaves. In Japan particularly well-marked variegated specimens of the oriental *Cymbidium* species are highly prized, and are grown for their foliage rather than their flowers.

Inflorescence
Orchids bear their flowers in an inflorescence that at its most basic is a single-flowered stalk (in *Lycaste*, *Masdevallia* and many more) or a simple raceme with flowers usually opening from the base upwards, arising either from a lateral node, or terminally from the seasonal growth of sympodials. More complex branched structures are found in many epiphytic orchids, with some species of *Oncidium* producing panicles several metres in length. There are species of *Bulbophyllum* that produce a most curious structure, consisting of a flattened rachis with flowers arising on both sides. Many *Pleurothallis* species have pseudobulbs that are little more than a stalk for the solitary leaf. Because the inflorescence arises from the apex of this pseudobulb, it often appears to be growing from the middle of the leaf.

Flowers
The basic structure of an orchid flower is remarkably consistent for such a large and diverse family. If we imagine that orchids evolved from some primitive lily-like ancestor, then we can see where the orchids diverged. The main segments are arranged in threes, as with lilies. The outer segment consists of three sepals with one uppermost and the other two symmetrically held left and right. As with other flowers the sepals form the outer protective covering of the developing bud and are green at this stage. However, unlike a typical 'ordinary' flower, the sepals of orchids, like those of lilies and others, take on colour as the flower opens, and become an integral part of the bloom, alongside the petals. The three sepals are usually similar to each other, although there are some remarkable exceptions, for example *Oncidium papilio*, where the dorsal sepal is similar to the petals and quite unlike the other two sepals. The lower two sepals are sometimes fused to form a single structure, as in some species of *Pleurothallis*. In the genus *Masdevallia* the flower is dominated by the three sepals, which are fused for much of their length to form an expanding tube with three tails, the other floral parts being quite small and almost lost inside.

Inside the three sepals are the three, usually highly coloured, petals, arranged to fill the three spaces between the sepals. Here the symmetry breaks down, because the petal opposite the dorsal sepal differs, often considerably, from the other two. This modified petal is known as the lip (or labellum), and gives the orchid flower its characteristic form. It often provides a landing platform for a visiting insect pollinator, but in some species it takes on a more active role in pollination.

The lip is often three-lobed, with, in the case of cattleyas and their relatives, the outer lobes rolled into a tube enclosing the column. Some lips are flat and warty, some are fringed or covered with hairs, while others have finely hinged appendages that, in the slightest breeze, are in constant motion. The lip of the slipper orchids (*Paphiopedilum*) takes on the characteristic pouch shape, and in the *Coryanthes* this container fills with liquid. Within the large orchid family there exists almost every conceivable shape of lip.

The base of the lip is often elongated backward to form a tube at the end of which is nectar. The length of this tube is directly related to the length of the proboscis of the pollinating insect, often a butterfly or a moth. Many native European orchids have these spurs, particularly the *Platanthera* species. There are many tropical orchids, particularly from Africa, that have very extended nectaries, and these flowers are also often white in colour and night-scented to encourage pollination by moths. The popular species *Angraecum sesquipedale* from Madagascar has a spur that is over 12in (30cm) long. When Charles Darwin saw this flower he predicted that there existed in Madagascar a huge moth with a proboscis of the same length. At the time no such moth was known, and his suggestion was ridiculed by entomologists. Unfortunately Darwin did not live long enough to see the discovery of the moth or to learn of its naming as *Xanthopan morgani praedicta* in honour of his prediction.

At the centre of the orchid flower is the single reproductive organ known as the column, which combines the male and female parts, the stamens and stigma, of other flowers. The structure of the column is basically quite simple and common to all orchids, but it has been contorted into a wide and bizarre range of forms by millennia of orchid evolution. On the underside of the column, near the end, is a concave sticky area – the stigmatic surface or female part. At the end of the column, separated from the stigmatic surface by a flap of tissue called the rostellum, are the male anthers. The pollen of orchids is not powdery but the individual grains are formed into two, four, six, or eight waxy masses, called pollinia, which are attached by a stalk called a stipe to a sticky pad called a viscidium. This whole congregation (pollinia, stipites, and viscidia) called the pollinarium, is enclosed in an anther cap. The number of pollinia and the exact structure, shape, and disposition of the elements of the column form the basis of the botanical classification of the orchid family.

Behind the flower is the ovary, in which will develop the seeds if the orchid flower is pollinated. Because the ovary is behind or below the sepals and petals it is said to be inferior. Orchids do not invest unnecessary effort in the development of the ovary prior to pollination, so it is often little more than a stalk behind the flower, with little differentiation between it and the true stalk, or pedicel. At the bud stage most orchid flowers have the lip uppermost, adjacent to the spike. As the flower opens, the pedicel twists so that the lip is at the bottom of the open flower. This process is known as resupination, and is common but not universal.

3

THE LIFE OF ORCHIDS

Reproduction

Most orchids reproduce vegetatively to some extent, and a few rely on this method almost exclusively, rarely resorting to flowers. Many terrestrials in temperate climates produce a tuber to carry them over a less-favourable season, and sometimes they will produce more than one. Some produce underground runners that give rise to separate individuals and eventually to extensive colonies. Epiphytes, both monopodials and sympodials, can spread theoretically indefinitely, and as they branch and the older parts of the plant die off they create separate individuals.

All these vegetative methods are asexual and produce offspring that are genetically identical. In an ecologically stable situation this may have some advantages, but a slight change in the environment can spell disaster for the colony. A population of slightly varied individuals, all members of the same species, may well have some members better able to cope with such a change, and although there may be a setback for the colony, if some individuals can survive, then the colony has a long-term future. Moreover the significant trait that the surviving minority possessed then becomes the norm as the population recovers, and the new colony is better able to cope should the problem recur. Variation results from a mixing of the genes, which is, however, only produced by sexual reproduction, and the variation thus produced is its great and important advantage. Without variation there can be no natural selection, and without natural selection there is no evolution.

Pollination

Most plant species are isolated either geographically or by genetic incompatibility. The bees in our gardens transfer pollen indiscriminately from species to species but we do not find hybrids between dahlias and delphiniums or between geraniums and gentians. Were it to happen then they would soon loose their identity in a hybrid swarm, and nature would be in a desperate mess. Where closely related species of plants can be induced to produce hybrids, as for instance with some species roses, we can be certain that in nature the individual species are well separated geographically, or in some cases perhaps flowers are borne at different seasons of the year.

A major and significant difference with orchids is that genetic compatibility between related species, and often between quite distantly related species, is the norm. It is common for pollen from one species to be able to fertilize another. But the world is not full of natural orchid hybrids, although there are a few, so there must be other effective methods of species isolation. It is the evolution of these barriers that has given rise to the unique structure of the orchid flower, and the wonderful and varied ways in which pollination is effected.

The two major objectives for an effective mechanism are firstly that pollen is transferred only to the stigma of a flower of the same species, and secondly that it is preferably not the same flower or a flower on the same plant. The ingenious ways in which this is achieved are as numerous and varied as the orchids themselves.

Orchids initially attract insects by a variety of

means. The flowers may be visually attractive, perhaps arousing some sense of curiosity, or more often by promising some reward. Colour plays an important part with many flowers, although it is fair to say that insects do not see colour as we do. They are very sensitive to ultra-violet light, which we do not see, and many flowers reveal unseen patterns when photographed using ultra-violet sensitive film. These unseen patterns of colour, and also much of the visible patterning, are designed to draw the attention of the insect to the centre of the flower where the patterns and structure of the lip encourage it towards the column. Butterflies see the colour red, whereas bees do not. Many red orchids also have narrow throats (for the butterfly's long thin proboscis) and small light pollinia which stick to the proboscis.

Scent is important in many orchids, and is not always pleasant to us. Many orchids are scented only at certain times of the day or night and so specific are some that one can almost set one's clock by them. Night-scented orchids are usually white and often have nectar-bearing spurs because all these three adaptations are directed towards pollination by moths.

Some orchids practise deception. Unpleasant and even revolting odours imitate rotting flesh or dung, and the flowers are usually appropriately coloured and even appropriately textured, particularly on the lip. Carrion flies and the like are attracted, and the stimulus is so convincing that the insects lay their eggs. As they do so in the inviting throat of the flower, the pollinarium is attached to their rear end, to be transferred later to another flower. The clever time delay to avoid self-pollination is, in this case, the time needed for the insect to manufacture another batch of eggs. Naturally the eggs perish, so in this case the relationship between orchid and insect has a definite loser. Presumably the deception is just good enough to ensure pollination for the orchid, but not so good that all the insects are fooled all the time. If they were, the orchid would soon have no pollinators and would become the victim of its own success. The system is self-regulating because those flies that were easily fooled all the time did not produce surviving offspring to inherit the trait, and those that were rarely or never fooled produced most

of the next generation, so the flies get cleverer. Likewise orchids that are too convincing reduce or wipe out their own pollinators and those not good enough are not pollinated. So, gradually over time, the orchids also get cleverer at the same pace as the flies – an example of the fine and subtle balance of an evolving and self-regulating system reliant on the exercise of natural selection.

Insects are rarely attracted to only one species of flower, so powdery pollen will not do for orchids. Instead, they produce pollinia, attached through a stalk, or stipe, to a sticky pad called the viscidium, the whole structure covered by the anther cap. When the flower is ready, the viscidium protrudes slightly from beneath the anther cap, and will stick firmly to a visiting insect. As the insect withdraws it removes the pollinia, firmly attached to some part of its anatomy, and the anther cap is dislodged. Self-pollination is prevented by a variety of ingenious means, usually involving some form of time delay. In some species the rostellum, the flap of tissue between the anther and the stigmatic surface, covers the stigma and folds back only some time after the pollen has been removed. In others the stigma is not sticky or receptive until some time later. Yet others give the insect some form of unpleasant experience, perhaps temporary imprisonment or an un-ceremonious dunking. The startled insect withdraws, returning to a similar flower only when it has regained its confidence, or the flower's attraction proves powerful enough to overcome fear. That insects do have some form of memory we know from the behaviour of honey bees in communicating the location of nectar-bearing flowers to others, and in returning to the flowers themselves. Perhaps the success of many orchids owes something to the length of that memory – long enough to minimize self-pollination by discouraging a quick return to a similar nearby flower, but not so long that the pollinia have deteriorated or the other flowers have faded before the insect recovers its nerve.

Porroglossum echidnum, a small orchid from South America, springs quite a surprise on the visiting insect. The lip is hinged at the base and when the insect lands it springs upward, trapping the insect against the underside of the column. The structure of the flower is such that the insect cannot retreat but must struggle forward, and in so doing first deposits any pollen which it is carrying on the stigma, and then, as it pushes out, it picks up another load in exactly the same position on its back. After such a shock the insect is presumably unlikely to repeat the experience immediately, and so is unlikely to return to a flower nearby. Cross-pollination with another plant rather than pollination of another flower on the same plant is thereby encouraged.

The same species of insect is often involved in the pollination of several species of orchid. Hybridization between different species of orchid is avoided by depositing the pollinia on different parts of the insect's body. Species of euglossine bee have been observed carrying pollinia from as many as fifteen different species of orchid in various positions on their backs, undersides, heads, legs, antennae, and mouthparts and even stuck to the unfortunate insect's eye. However, the orchid flowers concerned are structured in such a particular way that the visiting insect is forced to adopt a position that guarantees the correct pollen being deposited on the correct stigma.

Considerable violence is employed by members of the South American genus *Catasetum*. All species have the habit of producing two quite different types of flowers, one type being male and the other female. These are borne on spikes of either one or the other. The male flowers have two triggers that, when touched, cause the pollinarium to be ejected, viscidium first, with considerable force, sticking firmly to whatever gets in the way.

The more primitive sub-family of orchids consists of the four genera of slipper orchids, all of which have pouch- or slipper-shaped lips. Pollinating insects visit these flowers in pursuit of nectar, although none appears to be produced, and enter the pouch via the large opening. Once inside it is difficult for the insect to exit the same way. The pouches of some species have inside surfaces that are slippery, or covered with downward-pointing hairs, and in many cases the pouch is curved inward around the main entrance. At the rear of the pouch, however, there are often hairs designed to assist the insect's progress, or at least a surface that affords a foothold. As a result the insect is encouraged to make its way out via one of the two gaps at either side of the

column, pushing first against the stigmatic surface, depositing any pollen it may already be carrying, and then against one of the two pollen masses conveniently located at the tightest point of the exit. The pollen is solid and sticky but not arranged in discreet masses, or pollinia, as in other orchids, so several visiting insects can exit with some pollen. Unless the insect wishes to repeat the experience again with the same flower, self-pollination is avoided. Most slipper orchids produce one flower only per stem, but if more are produced the flowers usually open sequentially, so the insect must go elsewhere.

The most ingenious of all the trap flowers is found in the South and Central American genus *Coryanthes*. Several species produce bucket-shaped lips that encourage the insect pollinator to exit by pushing through a tight gap, first past the stigmatic surface, and then past the rostellum, removing the pollinarium in the process. Although the inside of the bucket is slippery, the entrance to the bucket is quite wide enough for the insect to simply fly back out the way it entered. However this is ingeniously prevented because the bucket is partly filled with liquid, secreted by the flower. With wet wings the insect cannot take off from the surface of the liquid, so it struggles to the side, eventually discovering the exit route.

There are many more examples of the great variety of ways in which orchids ensure their pollination, but a final and perhaps supreme example must be native European members of the genus *Ophrys*. These orchids employ the strongest of all driving forces – sex.

The common names of bee orchid, fly orchid and spider orchid refer to the resemblance of their convex lips to the bodies of various insects, an illusion often reinforced by petals or other flower parts imitating other parts of an insect's anatomy. The members of this genus occur throughout southern and central Europe, with the greatest concentration in the Mediterranean region, where they are dormant during the summer, relying on their underground tubers, and grow during the mild winter to flower in the spring. Britain represents the northern limit of their distribution, and here the same species produce a very much smaller plant which is often monocarpic (flowering once and then dying).

These orchids are not all pollinated by the insects suggested by their common names. They are pollinated by various species of solitary bees and wasps, each orchid species employing the services of just one species of insect. This exclusiveness is not quite absolute, so there are several hybrids reported, maybe due to an incompletely evolved system. Pollination is achieved by a most effective use of subterfuge by the orchid. In early spring the male insects emerge several weeks before the rather less numerous females. This ensures that the females are met by plenty of enthusiastic males. To attract them, the females emit a powerful chemical, or pheromone. The orchid produces its flowers during the few weeks immediately before the female insects emerge, and not only do they look like a receptive female but they also give off the same pheromone, or at least near enough to fool the males who, after all, have yet to experience the real thing. In attempting to mate with the flowers the male insects transfer pollen from one flower to another, by a process known as pseudocopulation.

Having seen a few of the many ingenious ways in which orchids have evolved to ensure cross-pollination, it is surprising to find several species that appear to rely, to a greater or lesser extent, on self-pollination. The European bee orchid (*Ophrys apifera*) appears to be exclusively self-pollinated in Britain, although perhaps less so further south in its distribution. Soon after the flower opens the pollinia fall out, hanging by their long and rather thin and flexible caudicles, the sticky viscidium remaining in place. Self-pollination is effected by the slightest breeze, which blows the hanging pollinia on to the stigmatic surface. In this case self-pollination may be an adaptation to the absence of the pollinator at the northern extreme of the population. This same explanation also seems appropriate in the case of several self-pollinating populations of species found in the West Indies, where the main populations are on the mainland of Central America, and are conventionally insect pollinated.

There are even orchids that take this process one stage further, not bothering to produce opening flowers at all but self-pollinating in the bud. This process is called cleistogamy, and is very common in the popular species *Cattleya aurantiaca*, which the collector should always purchase in flower to be sure that it is one that does produce opening flowers.

Seed and Germination

After pollination the column usually swells and envelops the captive pollinia. The other parts of the flower, and particularly the lip, often change colour before they wither away. At this stage the ovary is developing behind the flower, from what seemed to be merely the flower stalk, and is not actually fertilized until some time after pollination, in some cases three or more months later. Slowly each pollen grain grows a pollen tube down the inside of the column, and eventually fertilizes an ovum to produce a seed. In some species of *Phalaenopsis*, and others, the petals and sepals do not wither but remain fleshy and turn green, and by photosynthesis they take on the job of the leaves, presumably helping the development of the seed pod.

After a period varying with the species from a few weeks to many months, the seed pod ripens and splits to release the seeds. These are unusual in the plant world – there are very many of them and they are very small. Estimates vary, but at least three million have been reported from a single pod of the swan orchid *Cycnoches chlorochilon*. Being so small is obviously ideal for wind dispersal, an advantageous method particularly for epiphytes.

Most seeds consist of an embryo root, an embryo shoot, and a food reserve. However, orchid seeds are so small that they consist of only a few more or less undifferentiated cells and virtually no food reserves. On the face of it this presents the orchid with a serious problem. It solves it by an intricate strategy involving the cooperation of a fungus.

The term mycorrhiza refers to an apparently quite common symbiotic relationship between a fungus and the roots of a plant. The seeds of many trees germinate easily and grow for some time, initially on the food reserves in the seed, and later by photosynthesis. However, unless the roots encounter a particular fungus, and form a successful and permanent symbiotic relationship with it, the seedling will languish and die. Orchids must do this the other way round. The orchid seed has no food reserves and so needs the fungus at the point of germination, and can later do without it if necessary.

The dry seed first absorbs water and swells, splitting the seed coat. At this point the appropriate fungus must be present and must invade the cells in the embryo. The cells of the embryo then divide and form a small mass of undifferentiated cells called a protocorm, digesting the invading fungus as they multiply. At this early stage survival for the orchid hangs in the balance. Many are killed by the fungus and some get over-enthusiastic and digest all the fungus. For a few the relationship works well, each keeping the other in check, and the protocorm develops to the size of a pin head or larger and turns green. As photosynthesis commences the orchid becomes less dependent on the fungus. As the multiplying cells start to differentiate, a shoot forms at the top, and hairs and later roots form at the base of this shoot. From this point on we have what is recognizably a plant, which, as it grows stronger,

gradually relegates the fungus to its roots only, where it is found in mature orchids.

This whole process from seed to maturity may take many years – in the case of some European terrestrials fifteen years is reported – and particularly in the early stages is fraught with hazards. The complex biology of the orchids results in a fine population balance. Most orchids are long-term perennials, if somewhat slow growing, with reliable vegetative methods of multiplication. They have highly developed and effective strategies of sexual reproduction that maximize the advantages of evolution and produce millions of easily dispersed seeds. Balanced against this is the complexity of the pollination mechanism, which often results in few mature seed pods, and the biology of germination and early development is so tenuous that very few seeds or seedlings survive.

4
ORCHID NAMES

There are many examples among the orchids of reasonably well-known and well-used common names. Orchids of the genus *Phalaenopsis* are often referred to as moth orchids, and such naming is unlikely to cause confusion. *Cycnoches* are known as swan orchids and *Coryanthes* as bucket orchids. However, the vast majority of orchids do not have common names, and many of the common names may be well known locally but not internationally. *Oncidium papilio* from South America is often referred to as the butterfly orchid, but then so are the European species *Platanthera chlorantha* and *Platanthera bifolia*. It is therefore important that we use an internationally accepted system of nomenclature.

Most gardeners will be familiar with the binominal system of nomenclature that gives every plant a Latin genus name followed by a Latin specific name. They will be familiar, too, with the epithet that refers to a particular cultivar within the species. All this applies to orchids. Complications arise only when we come to consider orchid hybrids. As we have seen, orchids have evolved lacking much of the genetic incompatibility we find with most plants. Their intricate and ingenious pollination mechanisms restrict hybridization in the wild to a minimum, although natural hybrids do occur – several species of European marsh orchids in the genus *Dactylorhiza* hybridize with each other so readily that it is rare to find a population without hybrids. This makes identification of individuals almost impossible and leads to experts producing various different classifications of the same genus. The easiest way to annoy a European orchid en-

thusiast is to ask him positively to identify a marsh orchid!

Because orchids are genetically compatible, orchid growers soon discovered that they could produce artificial hybrids between species in the same genus, and as the results were often fertile, so the process could continue. There are other plant genera where hybrids can be made between some species, often producing only sterile offspring, but no other plants approach the ease with which orchids are prepared to oblige. Where the orchids are almost unique is that it is possible to produce artificial hybrids between species of different genera, called intergeneric hybrids, and surprisingly these are also often fertile. Furthermore, this compatibility is not confined only to very closely related genera, and we should not be surprised to find even the odd hybrid, in this case almost certainly sterile, between members of different tribes.

The nomenclature of hybrids is different from species and is controlled by different, but just as strict a set of rules as species, again to avoid confusion. Let us take as an example a hybrid *Cattleya*, which we might make and raise to maturity using two species, *Cattleya dowiana* from Costa Rica and Colombia, and *Cattleya gaskelliana* from Venezuela. The name of this hybrid will be *Cattleya* Lord Rothschild. This hybrid was first made by Sanders, the famous orchid firm, and registered by them when it flowered in 1893, and presumably named by them in honour of one of their valued customers. If we, or anyone else, makes another hybrid with any plants of the same two species, even if a different variety of one or other is used, and whichever acts as male or female, then all the offspring, however variable they may be, must bear this hybrid name.

The same rule applies if the parents are hybrids. *Cattleya* Amantic was made by Charlesworths, another famous orchid firm, and registered in 1932. The parents were *Cattleya* Lord Rothschild and *Cattleya* President Wilson. If we make a hybrid with any *Cattleya* Lord Rothschild, and as with all hybrids they were all probably quite different from each other, with any *Cattleya* President Wilson, then all the offspring are called *Cattleya* Amantic, no matter how different from each other they may turn out to be.

The records indicate that *Cattleya* Lord Rothschild was a fine hybrid. Individual plants appear in the awards records with various owners, each with its further individual cultivar epithet. For instance *Cattleya* Lord Rothschild 'Fairy Queen' was given an Award of Merit by the Royal Horticultural Society when it was exhibited by Charlesworths in 1932. Maybe this fine individual was the parent of the original *Cattleya* Amantic, or maybe another *Cattleya* Lord Rothschild was used. The name *Cattleya* Amantic would apply regardless. Of course we are perfectly entitled to differentiate the offspring of our remake of the same hybrid by giving each a further name if we wish.

Intergeneric hybrids create a different set of problems, almost unique to orchids, because we have in effect created a new genus. We have combined two genera to produce a bigeneric hybrid, so not only do we need a new name for the hybrid as before, but we also need a new name for the newly created genus. These new generic names are compound names constructed from the generic names of the parents. Thus the hybrid between *Brassavola digbyana* and *Cattleya dowiana* is *Brassocattleya* Mrs J. Leemann, again with the generic name in italics. Any hybrid produced from any *Brassavola* (species or hybrid) crossed with any *Cattleya* (species or hybrid), either way round, would produce a hybrid in the genus *Brassocattleya*. Also, if a *Brassocattleya* was crossed with a *Cattleya* or a *Brassavola*, or the other way round, the result will still be a *Brassocattleya*. A *Laelia* crossed with a *Cattleya* produces a

Laeliocattleya, so hopefully the origin of a *Brassolaelia* is now obvious.

In 1921 Charlesworths registered the result of a hybrid between *Laeliocattleya* Artemis and *Brassocattleya* Mrs J. Leemann. This is *Brassolaeliocattleya* Camada, a trigeneric hybrid. Once again this generic name applies to hybrids from members of the three genera *Brassavola*, *Laelia*, and *Cattleya* in any combination. It may be as in this example or it may be a hybrid between a *Brassolaelia* and a *Cattleya*. In the course of all this hybridizing the related genus *Sophronitis*, a delightful genus of several small orchids with startlingly bright red flowers, was introduced to bring its colour to the hybrids. So, we had *Sophrolaelia* and *Sophrocattleya* and all the other possible permutations, and the commercial nurserymen had a field day.

In 1916 Charlesworths registered *Sophrolaeliocattleya* Isabella, another trigeneric hybrid, and twelve years later registered the result of a hybrid between this and their *Brassolaeliocattleya* Camada. This produced a quadrigeneric hybrid which they registered as Camella and which we might imagine is going to have the ridiculous name of *Brassosophrolaeliocattleya*. Fortunately, at some point someone realized where it might all lead, and common sense took over. The genus *Potinara* was established in 1922 for these quadrigeneric hybrids. All hybrids that involve four or more genera, and most of those that involve three, have generic names usually derived from the name of some significant person, with the suffix *ara* added. Compound generic names are now usually confined to bigeneric hybrids, and some trigeneric instances where the combined result is convenient.

There are examples of naturally occurring hybrids and even, rarely, of naturally occurring intergeneric hybrids. In such cases the nomenclature is as if it were a species, with a letter × before the second name, for example *Cymbidium* × *ballianum*. If we were to make that hybrid artificially, then we would write it as *Cymbidium* Ballianum. If we had made such a hybrid before the botanists had discovered and named the natural equivalent, then we would have had to give it a non-latin name, as with all artificial hybrids. The botanists would then have to find another name, in Latin, for their discovery, although it would be the same hybrid. In the case of a rare natural intergeneric hybrid then the same applies, but this time without the ×. The hybrid generic name is used, for example *Laeliocattleya leeana*.

There are official abbreviations for all the generic names and these are usually reasonably obvious. For example *C.* for *Cattleya*, *Cym.* for *Cymbidium*, and *Blc.* for *Brassolaeliocattleya*. In addition to these it is permitted to use a single letter, for example *C.* for *Cymbidium*, when the context precludes any possibility of confusion with any other genus.

Abbreviations of orchid generic names used in the colour plate section

C.	*Cattleya*	*Odm.*	*Odontoglossum*
Cirr.	*Cirrhopetalum*	*Odtna.*	*Odontonia*
Coel.	*Coelogyne*	*Onc.*	*Oncidium*
Cym.	*Cymbidium*	*Paph.*	*Paphiopedilum*
Den.	*Dendrobium*	*Phal.*	*Phalaenopsis*
Epc.	*Epicattleya*	*Phrag.*	*Phragmipedium*
Lc.	*Laeliocattleya*	*Pptm.*	*Propetalum*
Lyc.	*Lycaste*	*Rhrds.*	*Rhynchorides*
Masd.	*Masdevallia*	*Sand.*	*Sanderara*
Max.	*Maxillaria*	*Slc.*	*Sophrolaeliocattleya*
Milt.	*Miltonia*	*Soph.*	*Sophronitis*
Mtssa.	*Miltassia*	*Vuyl.*	*Vuylstekeara*
Oda.	*Odontioda*	*Wils.*	*Wilsonara*
Odcdm.	*Odontocidium*	*Zyg.*	*Zygopetalum*

5

HISTORY

The word orchid comes originally from the Greek *orchis*, meaning testis, and refers to the resemblance of the paired tubers of many Mediterranean species to the testicles. Although orchids had then been grown for some two thousand years in China, the term was first used by the Greek scientist Theophrastus in the fourth century BC.

The earliest introductions to Britain may well have been of European species, but the first record from far afield is to be found in *Theatricum Botanicum*, published in 1640 and written by John Parkinson, royal herbalist to Charles I. In this work appears an illustration of an orchid, probably *Cypripedium acaule*, which had been introduced into cultivation from North America some time before.

As many parts of the world were explored and conquered by Europeans, particularly during the 16th and 17th centuries, the great beauty of tropical orchids came in the form of reports and illustrations, and dried specimens of orchids began to be sent back home by European settlers overseas. Many of the early introductions of orchids, particularly during the 18th century, were as a result of settlers sending specimens back to Europe, often to their relatives. As soon as interest was stirred, merchants began to involve themselves in the beginnings of what was to become the extensive orchid trade of the next century.

The first tropical orchid to flower in Europe was *Brassavola nodosa*, introduced from Central America at the end of the 17th century. It flowered in Holland and was illustrated in Paul Hermann's *Paradisus Batavus*, which was published in 1698.

The first to flower in England was *Bletia verecunda*, sent in 1731 from the Bahamas as a dried specimen to Peter Collinson, a cloth merchant. On discovering that there were some signs of life left, he took it to Sir Charles Wager, who plunged it in a bed of bark in one of his hot houses for the winter. The following spring it produced leaves, in the summer it flowered – and in all probability promptly died. It was recorded in *Historia Plantarum Rariorum* by John Martyn, published in 1732.

During the next few decades a few successful attempts to introduce exotic species were recorded, particularly from the Caribbean and Central America. Vanilla was grown for a time, and a few *Epidendrum* species were introduced, some even surviving long enough to flower. Interest was stimulated progressively during the 18th century by an increasing number of published reports and illustrations of exotic orchids from an increasing number of missionaries, travellers, and explorers.

Attempts were made, on an increasing scale, to cultivate these exotics in the greenhouses of the time, but always with little success. In 1778 Dr John Fothergill introduced to Britain *Cymbidium ensifolium* and *Phaius tankervilleae* from China, and in 1787 two species of *Encyclia* flowered at the Royal Botanic Gardens, Kew. By 1794 only fifteen species of exotic orchids are recorded as in cultivation at Kew, with very few of them being tropical in origin.

In 1810, the *Botanical Magazine* reported that a Mr Watson, later to become well known as an authority on the cultivation of orchids, and at the time gardener to a Mr Woodford, was having considerable success with slipper orchids. At this time there were some small private collections being maintained by wealthy individuals in London and in the north of England around Manchester and Liverpool. Much early trade with the New World came through the port of Liverpool, and the botanic garden there became famous for its collection of exotics, including orchids. The early interest was so concentrated in the north that it was the Manchester and North of England Orchid Society that first began to give awards to orchids, even before the Royal Horticultural Society in London.

Perhaps, with hindsight, we can say that the most significant introduction came in 1818, and as with so many important events, it happened by chance. On a visit to Brazil, William Swainson collected a number of plants from the Organ Mountains around Rio de Janeiro to send back to England, and used some 'tough stems and leaves' as packing material. Some of this consignment found its way to William Cattley, who was so intrigued by the curious swollen stems of this packing material, some of which appeared to be still alive, that he potted some up, and placed them in his greenhouse. From among the resulting plants he successfully flowered *Cattleya labiata* later that year, and was amazed by the beauty of this quite unknown orchid. The first *Cattleya* had been introduced some years earlier, and had been flowering regularly at Liverpool Botanic Garden under the name of *Epidendrum violaceum*, but had not been particularly noticed. William Cattley's new orchid created quite a stir, and undoubtedly heralded the start of orchid growing as a fashionable pastime for the wealthy. His collection soon became the largest in private hands, and in 1820, on the recommendation of Joseph Hooker, he employed the young botanist John Lindley to write about his collection of exotic plants. This work was published in 1821 as *Collecteano Botanico*.

Around 1833 the Duke of Devonshire, whose gardens at Chatsworth in Derbyshire under head gardener Joseph Paxton were among the finest in England, saw his first exotic orchid, *Oncidium papilio*, at an exhibition. He was immediately captivated and set about collecting orchids as soon as they became available. He built and extended the hot houses at Chatsworth to accommodate the growing collection, but it was soon clear that a new structure was required. In 1836 building started on a great conservatory, designed for the Duke by Paxton, which soon became the marvel of the age. During these years the Duke spent lavishly on his orchid collection, and was the single most significant factor in the growth and prosperity of the orchid firms of the day. These firms were eventually able to send collectors around the world for new orchids, in the early days often sponsored by the Duke, but still the Duke's appetite could not be satisfied. In 1835, at the suggestion of Paxton, he sent John Gibson, a young gardener working at Chatsworth, to India to collect orchids.

By 1847 the Chatsworth collection was the finest in Britain, and we remember this period in the names of many orchids, not least the three dendrobiums named after the three main characters in the story: *Dendrobium devonianum*, *D. paxtonii*, and *D. gibsonii*.

The work at Chatsworth covered an important time in the development of the orchidomania that was to sweep Europe and, eventually, America. This golden age coincided with the reign of Queen Victoria and began in 1837 – a year in which orchids were sent to Europe from Mexico, from Guiana, from Guatemala, and from the Philippines. James Bateman wrote in the preface to his book *Orchidaceae of Mexico and Guatemala*, that 'probably three hundred species were seen in England for the first time in that memorable year'.

As the obsession with orchids gradually gained momentum among the wealthy, the demand for new and exciting discoveries exceeded supply. The great orchid nurseries of Bull, Rollinson, Low, and Veitch in England and Linden in Brussels, were founded on this apparently insatiable demand. All orchids soon found a ready market, but the particular requirement was for new discoveries, which might then be named in honour of the owner.

The firm of Veitch was founded at the beginning of the century, but it was with James Veitch that we associate the growing of orchids. He was born in 1815 and served his apprenticeship at Rollinsons nursery, where he first encountered orchids. When he later moved to the family firm a number of orchids moved with him, a phenomenon which is not unknown to this day, and formed the basis of the firm's stock of orchids. In 1840, following the trend established by the Duke of Devonshire, Veitch sent William Lobb to collect orchids in Chile, Peru, and Brazil, and in 1843 William's brother Thomas was sent to India and Burma for the same purpose. These two brothers were the first commercial orchid hunters.

Within a few years there were professional collectors scouring the jungles of the world for new treasures, and over the next half century their successes made handsome fortunes for their employers. Several are immortalized in the names of many of our most popular orchids. However, the finest of their discoveries were rather more likely to end up with names that honoured their employers, or their employers' more important customers! A few of these courageous adventurers survived to retire, but none shared the fortunes their successes generated, and many perished, often so early in their careers that they remain anonymous.

At the height of the mania the firm of Sanders had upwards of twenty full time collectors in the field at the same time, and in total there must have been hundreds of these intrepid souls surviving on their wits in the remotest corners of the world. There are many stories of orchid hunting, some amusing, some heroic and many tragic. There were stories of collectors, working for rival establishments, who met on the same ship on the outward journey, both in pursuit of the same orchid. Some found themselves following each other through the jungle, often following the same false trail set by yet another collector. Rumour and false rumour abounded in what was a highly competitive business.

Perhaps the most notable member of this profession was Benedict Roezl, who was born in 1823 in Prague, in what was then Bohemia. He was employed by Sanders for forty years, during which time he crossed and re-crossed North, Central, and South America many times, always alone and usually on foot. Earlier in his life he had lost his left hand whilst demonstrating a piece of machinery of his own invention, and in its place he wore an iron hook. This proved to be fascinating to the native tribes with whom he spent so much of his life, and indeed their awe of it may have contributed to his survival. Late in life he retired to live in Prague, where he died in 1885. Such was his fame that his lavish funeral was attended by many dignitaries, amongst them the Kaiser, and a statue was erected to his memory. He is credited with having discovered 800 species of plants, several of them familiar orchids, and is remembered in many of their names.

As competition increased throughout the 19th century, so collectors became more concerned not only to ensure their own success, but where possible to thwart their rivals. Forests were stripped of orchids and often then clear-felled to ensure that none were left for competitors to find. Soon consignments of ten thousand plants of a single species were commonplace, and in 1878 William Bull was able to announce the arrival of two shipments of orchids that he estimated to contain two million plants. Concern about the vast numbers involved was expressed as early as 1850 when B. S. Williams wrote that collectors were 'ransacking the forests' in the pursuit of ever more orchids.

On their arrival in Europe the orchids were sorted, graded, and offered for sale by auction at Messrs Stevens, and later also at Messrs Prothero and Morris. So long as demand continued to grow then prices continued to rise, with large sums, often hundreds of pounds, changing hands for rarities or for new introductions. Most plants were rather sorry sights after their long journey, but there were many purchasers prepared to gamble on the identity of these supposed new rarities, and indeed prepared to gamble on their survival.

As time passed more and more information was forthcoming from the collectors concerning the climatic conditions in which orchids were found. Collectors were increasingly required by their employers to provide as much information as possible, and with it came the realization that many of the finest types grew in quite cool areas of the tropics. For too long it had been assumed that the tropics were universally hot and wet. It was not grasped that climate depended on altitude just as much as latitude. Around the middle of the century Paxton wrote in his *Magazine of Botany* urging that the highlands of Mexico and South America be scoured for new, cool-growing species, so that the growing of orchids could be brought within the means of a wider public. Choice specimens and superior varieties continued to fetch high prices, but the price of relatively common species tumbled as ever more were imported.

In 1851 a series of influential articles, entitled 'Orchids for the Millions,' appeared in the *Gardeners' Chronicle*. They were written by Benjamin Williams, an orchid grower who founded the wonderfully named Victoria and Paradise Nurseries in London a decade later. His articles focussed on the culture of these new cool-growing species, emphasising the importance of fresh air and light. They immediately struck a chord, and provided an enormous boost to the trade as more and more of the emerging middle class sought the status that an orchid collection conferred on its owner. In 1852 these articles on cultivation were assembled as *The Orchid Growers' Manual*, which became an instant best seller and was progressively enlarged through several editions. The last, and best known was the seventh edition, enlarged, after Williams' death in 1890, by his son, and published in 1894. Williams influenced the popularizing of orchids more than any other individual. The introduction to his book starts 'The cultivation of Orchidaceous plants is no longer exclusively the privilege of the few ...'. It is interesting to reflect that among the many misconceptions still popularly held about orchids, the one that associates them with exclusivity and wealth is still so widely believed that I might well have felt the need to start this book with the same comment.

In 1847 the Reverend William Herbert, Dean of Manchester, wrote in the *Journal* of the Horticultural Society of London that he had produced seed pods by pollinating species of *Orchis* with pollen from another species of *Orchis*, but had been unable to take the experiment further. He wrote that the 'cross breeding among Orchidaceous plants would perhaps lead to very startling results; but, unfortunately, they are not easily raised from seed'. Two years later Dr F.W. Moore, curator of the Royal Botanic Garden at Glasnevin, Dublin, wrote an article in the *Gardeners' Chronicle* entitled 'On Growing Orchid from Seeds'. He did not say whether these successes had been from self-pollination or from cross-pollination, but he stressed the difficulty of keeping the small seedlings

alive in the early years of their growth. In the same year Robert Gallier reported in the same journal that he had obtained seed from a cross of *Dendrobium nobile* with the pollen of *Dendrobium chrysanthum*, but that the seedlings had soon died. The hybridization of orchids had begun.

One name that has remained synonymous with the development of orchid hybrids is that of John Dominy. Almost the whole of Dominy's working life was spent with the firm of Veitch, sometimes at their Chelsea nursery, but mostly at Exeter. During his time in Exeter he met a Dr John Harris, who was a frequent visitor to the nursery. Dr Harris had studied botany as part of his medical training, and he understood the peculiar structure of the orchid column, and its function. He pointed this out to John Dominy and suggested the possibility of orchid hybridization. With this encouragement Dominy began to experiment with cattleyas and other genera. The first hybrid seed to germinate was in fact *Cattleya guttata* × *Cattleya loddigesii*, which was made in 1853 and named as *Cattleya* × *hybrida* when it flowered in 1856. However, the honour of being the first hybrid to flower belongs to *Calanthe* × *dominyi* (we would now write it as *Calanthe* Dominyi), a cross between *Calanthe furcata* and *Calanthe masuca*, which was made in 1854 and flowered before the cattleya in 1856.

This first orchid hybrid caused quite a stir, not only among collectors and enthusiasts but also among botanists. They were already wrestling with the enormously complex problems of orchid classification, and the prospect of orchid 'mules', as hybrids were then known, was hardly welcome. John Lindley's famous remark when he saw this first hybrid was 'You will drive the botanists mad!'

In 1859 Dominy exhibited five blooming plants of one of his early *Cattleya* hybrids at a London show. They were much admired, but they served as an early lesson for all hybridists as Dominy had forgotten to record their parentage. It was later decided that they were probably *Cattleya* Hybrida. In 1863 Dominy flowered the first intergeneric hybrid, a cross between *Cattleya mossiae* and *Laelia crispa*, which was named *Laeliocattleya* Exoniensis.

For over fifteen years the firm of Veitch was, thanks to the efforts of John Dominy, the only nursery to offer hybrids to the buying public. Many early experiments produced empty seed pods and, even when viable seed was obtained, germination proved difficult. Few seedlings were produced and, even though prices remained high, opinions as to their merits remained divided. Although when Dominy retired in 1880 his twenty-two years of hybridizing had produced most of the orchid hybrids around, they still numbered only twenty-five. His work at Veitch's nursery was continued by John Seden, who retired in 1905 having raised over 500 orchid hybrids during his career.

These early primary hybrids were variable and were intermediate between the parents in characteristics. Dr Lindley noticed this and suggested that perhaps some orchid species might in fact be natural hybrids, particularly those that were themselves quite variable. It had been suggested in the 18th century that several European terrestrial orchids appeared to produce hybrids intermediate in form between two recognized species. In 1852 a single plant in a consignment of *Phalaenopsis amabilis* proved to have flowers quite different from the others. Lindley had long suspected that this might be a natural hybrid between *Phalaenopsis amabilis* and *Phalaenopsis rosea* (now known as *Phalaenopsis equestris*), as the flowers were exactly intermediate in appearance. He wrote to Seden suggesting that he might try to make the hybrid, which he did. A single seedling survived to flower in 1892 and proved to be almost identical to the wild collected plant, which Lindley had named *Phalaenopsis intermedia*.

The latter part of the 19th century, the golden age of orchid growing, was dominated by Frederick Sander. He was born in Hanover, Germany, in 1847 and from an early age was fascinated by plants. As a young man he became concerned at the rise of Bismarck, and, still in his teens, he moved to England, where he worked in a nursery. During these years he met Benedict Roezl, an explorer and adventurer, who introduced him to orchids, and although Sander was twenty-four years younger than Roezl, their friendship and later business relationship was to last until Roezl's death in 1885. Sander began to import and sell orchids, many collected for him by Roezl, and soon became obsessed by them. He married well and with the help of

his wife's money was able to purchase a seed business in St Albans in 1876. He soon extended the business, building sheds in which to sort and distribute seeds and, increasingly, the large numbers of orchids he imported. In 1878, still trading as an agricultural seed merchant, he purchased some land alongside his premises, and commenced the building of what was to become the largest orchid nursery of the age. By 1885 the firm of Sanders had become Orchid Growers.

By 1891 Frederick Sander had reached the pinnacle of his fame. He presided over an orchid empire of hundreds of thousands of orchids housed in more than sixty greenhouses extending over several acres at St Albans. The site was served by its own railway siding, where consignments of orchids from his collectors around the world were delivered to be unpacked and sorted day and night. The aristocracy and the crowned heads of Europe could visit this temple to the orchid to make their purchases, arriving by train at the private, carpeted platform, to be met by Frederick Sander in top hat and tails. From this they could walk, via a long corridor, to the show greenhouses where the plants were arranged in vast artistic displays. The Romanoffs made him a Baron of the Holy Russian Empire and Queen Victoria appointed him Royal Orchid Grower. He was one of the original holders of the Royal Horticultural Society's Victoria Medal of Honour, and held many other foreign orders including the Belgian Order of the Crown and the French President's Prix d'Honneur. He won forty-one gold medals and was awarded too many cups, trophies, and diplomas to count. *Punch*, the popular magazine, crowned him 'The Orchid King'.

During the 1880's Sander opened a branch nursery at Summit, New Jersey, which was managed by Forstermann, one of his collectors. The great distance of this establishment from England proved too much of a problem, and it was sold in 1896 to John Lager and Henry Hurrell, both of whom had gained their experience of orchids in England. The firm of Lager & Hurrell was one of the pioneers of orchid growing in the United States of America, concentrating in the early years on cut-flower production, particularly white cattleyas and laelias for weddings.

In 1894 Sander began building a new nursery near

Bruges in Belgium. This establishment was soon much larger than that at St Albans, and at its height had over two hundred and fifty greenhouses filled with many different kinds of plants, with fifty or so devoted to orchids. Much of Sanders hybridizing and seedling raising was undertaken in Belgium.

If there is a secret to explain Frederick Sander's rapid rise to fame it must be his absolute devotion to his beloved orchids. His German extraction may have made him more acceptable to royalty, particularly to Queen Victoria, but in the early years of this century, as war loomed, it may have had the opposite effect, encouraging him to spend more time at Bruges. He had a knack of successfully guessing where the next new and valuable orchid might be found. He corresponded at great length with his collectors, often writing twice in the same day, and clearly commanded great loyalty and devotion. He was able to motivate them to succeed when they might otherwise abandon the search.

World War I brought irreversible changes to society in Europe, and many of the great collections were broken up. Fuel for heating was limited, and even when supplies were restored it was never again to be cheap. Labour was short during hostilities, and although the post-war years saw mass unemployment, there were few large private collections or commercial nurseries remaining, although some survived in a much-reduced form. During the early years of this century few new, and therefore commercially valuable, species were discovered and the commercial establishments suffered as the price of orchids at auction fell. The age of the orchid collection as a necessary status symbol of the wealthy was well and truly over.

Gradually nurserymen turned their attentions to raising orchids from seed, hoping to replace lucrative new species with equally spectacular new hybrids. Seed raising was rather haphazard, though gradually the technique of sowing seed around the mother plant was developed to the point of commercial viability. The first breakthrough was made by a Frenchman, Noel Bernard, who wrote a series of papers between 1903 and 1909 detailing his work with mycorrhizal fungi. He had isolated the fungus from the roots of orchids, and was the first to propose the symbiotic relationship between the

fungus and the orchid, suggesting that the orchid seed would germinate and grow only when the fungus was present. This work, together with that of Hans Burgeff, established that orchid seed could be germinated and grown in sterile flasks, on an agar jelly containing ground salep (the tubers of *Ophrys*) together with the fungus. Sterility was necessary because without it the orchid seedlings could not compete for the nutrients with the faster-growing colonies of moulds, fungi, and bacteria that soon infect the culture. Many orchid nurseries experimented with this new method, but it was the firm of Charlesworths who commenced the first scientific breeding programme, raising many thousands of *Odontoglossum* and *Odontioda* hybrids by this method.

The salep used in this method contained mainly starch, and it was argued by Dr Louis Knudson, a plant physiologist at Cornell University, that the function of the fungus was to break this down to the simple sugars needed by the germinating orchid. Knudson suggested, in a number of papers in the 1920s, that orchid seeds could be germinated and grown on a nutrient agar medium, without the presence of mycorrhizal fungi, if simple sugars like glucose and fructose were present. This method was proved in 1930, and was soon adopted by nurseries. It remains basically unchanged to this day, and the various formulations of agar, water, trace nutrients, and sugar are still often referred to as Knudson Formulae.

A major problem in orchid hybridization was that, even when the parents are carefully selected for their superior qualities, the proportion of good offspring was almost always low. The process of raising large quantities of seedlings to flowering in order to select a few was costly and time consuming, usually taking four to seven years. The few superior offspring did command high prices, and when they could be divided these propagations were also valuable, but orchids are slow to multiply, often producing only one division every other year. What was needed in orchid hybridization was a way to mass-produce these few superior hybrids, and this was eventually perfected in 1960 by Dr Georges Morel, director of the National Institute of Agricultural Research at Versailles, France.

At the tip of the dormant growth bud, known as the apical meristem, are a number of cells that are undifferentiated – that is, they are neither root cells nor shoot cells, although they have the potential to produce either. This apical meristem can be removed and, so long as it remains sterile, can be grown into a plant on agar, in much the same way as seed is germinated. This had been known for some time, and had been applied to other plants, but not to orchids. Dr Morel noted that these cells were free of virus, even when the rest of the plant was infected, and he succeeded in raising virus-free plants by this means. He also noticed that in the early stages of growth the undifferentiated cells often proliferated, eventually producing several identical plants rather than just one. Although he reported his findings in the *American Orchid Society Bulletin* in July 1960, the commercial possibilities escaped notice. In America Dr Donald Wimber was pursuing research in clonal multiplication at the Brookhaven National Laboratories, along similar lines to Dr Morel, and published his findings on 'Clonal Multiplication of Cymbidiums through Tissue Culture of the Shoot Meristem' in 1963. Still the commercial orchid establishments did not catch on. The next year Dr Morel stated clearly that proliferation could be induced artificially by disorientating the growing meristem, and that if it were divided it could go on indefinitely. He had already successfully flowered meristem-propagated plants of cymbidiums and miltonias, and had calculated that 'if each protocorm gives only four new ones per month, it is possible to obtain more than 4 million plants in a year from a single bud.' The commercial orchid trade now caught on!

In time orchid growing became a hobby of the emerging middle classes. More recently it has become a hobby for all classes. Today there is a new type of orchid enthusiast, with perhaps a few hundred orchid plants, many of them hybrids, in a modest greenhouse. The use of clonal multiplication has been extended to most orchid genera (paphiopedilums remain reluctant to cooperate), so the finest new hybrids are soon available to all at modest prices. Species are increasingly being raised from seed for the hobbyists, and there is little justification left for collecting from the wild, other than for genuinely scientific purposes.

Cym. Highland Canary
The latest in a long line of famous green standard cymbidiums bred by McBean's of England. Its parents are _Cym_. Cariga, which produced many large yellows that have won awards, and _Cym_. Mavourneen, an equally famous green cross. The large, clear, apple-green flowers are carried well on an upright spike in spring. As with all green cymbidiums the flowers should be shaded from direct sun to prevent the colour from fading to yellow.

Cym. Srinagar 'Plush'
Although more than twenty
years old, this fine cymbidium
(left) is still a favourite, with
medium-sized, clean blush-
pink flowers carried on a semi-
arching spike. It was bred in
Dorset from _Cym_. Chiron, a
deep olive green, and the
famous old hybrid _Cym_.
Rosanna, some of which were
white, and some a delicate
pink.

Cym. Lady McAlpine
A new standard pink hybrid
(above), bred by McBean's,
which flowers in mid-season,
producing large, pink-flushed
flowers on an upright stem. Its
parents are _Cym_. Howick, a
very large, 5in (12.5cm),
white, and _Cym_. York
Meredith, a fine yellow-green.
Both the parents have received
Awards of Merit from
Britain's Royal Horticultural
Society.

Cym. **Tanganyika 'Stripes Hill'**

Bred in America more than twenty-five years ago, this large-flowered standard is still well-thought-of, with its pink-flushed, cheerful yellow flowers carried well away from the stem. As cymbidiums are bred with ever larger flowers, there can be a tendency for crowding on the spike, which, in extreme cases, may prevent the flowers from turning or opening properly. A good long pedicel behind the flower helps to prevent these problems, and this is an important factor that, in the past, has not always been fully considered when parents were chosen for breeding.

Cym. Ayres Rock 'Mont Millais'

Really good, large-flowered red cymbidiums are rare, most being either deep pink or claret. This (above left) is undoubtedly one of the finest of the new generation. It was bred by McBean's and named after the well-known Australian landmark. The parents were *Cym*. Hamsey, a well-known red of years ago, and *Cym*. Rodkobb, a fine hybrid bred by the late Dr Borg in Finland.

Cym. Alexanderi 'Westonbirt'

When this most famous cymbidium first flowered just before World War I, Sir George Holford knew immediately that he had a winner. The cross was between a primary hybrid, *Cym*. Eburneo-lowianum, and a species, *Cym. insigne*, and produced white and cream offspring, with some having a pink flush. Various clones of this cross have won numerous awards, but 'Westonbirt' remains the most famous because it has produced so many fine offspring itself. Although is is rarely seen these days, its influence continues in almost all the modern cymbidiums – there are very few that cannot trace their ancestry back to this fine old white.

Cym. Jean Angus 'Apple Fair'

This is a miniature cymbidium with pendent or semi-pendent sprays of 2in (5cm) bright green flowers produced in spring from a compact plant. The parents of this cross were a medium-sized standard yellow, _Cym._ Caligold, and the small, multi-flowered Indian species _Cym. devonianum_. This is one of many hybrids from this species produced over many years in Dorset, England, by Keith Andrew.

***Cym.* Dag**

A favourite miniature
cymbidium, Dag (above left)
produces upright spikes of
clear green flowers in spring.
Miniature cymbidiums have
become increasingly popular
with growers, who find that
standard hybrids take up
rather a lot of space. They are
produced by breeding with
one or other of a number of
small-flowered species, and
have many of the
characteristics of whichever
miniature species is used.
Cym. Dag was bred some
years ago in America and
represents an early use of the
Oriental species *Cym. pumilum*
(now correctly *Cym.
floribundum*), mated with *Cym.*
Esmeralda, an old green
hybrid from *Cym. lowianum*.

***Cym.* Tiger Orb 'April'**

Cym. tigrinum comes from
Burma and Thailand and,
although it is a small plant
with short, wide leaves, it has
spikes of up to seven relatively
large yellow or bronze flowers
in early summer. Formerly
much neglected by breeders, it
has been used in recent years
to produce compact hybrids
that flower late and so extend
the cymbidium season. The
yellow colour of *Cym. tigrinum*
is very dominant in breeding,
and so far few notable hybrids
have been produced in other
colours. This orchid (above
right), as its name indicates,
flowers from April on, and was
the result of a cross between
the species and *Cym.*
Ormoulu, a fine old standard
yellow hybrid.

Cym. Lepe Green

A second-generation miniature cymbidium hybrid from the species *Cym. devonianum*, this (left) retains the pendulous, multi-flowered habit of its ancestor. Three different clones are shown: 'Dorset Green' in the centre is flanked by 'Plush Gold' and 'Mandarin'. The parents of *Cym.* Lepe Green were *Cym.* Sikkim Gold and *Cym.* Dryden, both hybrids from *Cym. devonianum*.

Cym. Minuet

This miniature cymbidium (above) is a primary hybrid – that is, a hybrid between two species. It was made almost half a century ago, by H. G. Alexander, and, as it was the first time the species *Cym. pumilum* had been used as a parent, it can reasonably be thought of as the first miniature cymbidium. It is still a firm favourite with its stiffly upright spikes of many pink flowers, well displayed all round the stem. The colour comes from the other parent, *Cym. insigne*, a large terrestrial species from Viet Nam.

Cym. Zaskar 'Silver Wedding'
This is a first-generation miniature cymbidium, recently bred in England, using *Cym. devonianum*, a small-flowered species from India. The delicate pink colour is inherited from the other parent, the blush-pink standard *Cym.* Srinagar 'Plush', and the dark lip markings come from the species. Although *Cym. devonianum* produces distinctly pendulous spikes, its offspring can be staked while in bud so that they open as gently arching sprays. Providing that this is done early enough, the buds of most orchids will adjust and the flowers will all open the right way up. Once they start to open they will not reorient themselves, and attention too late to this aspect of care produces ugly sprays of flowers.

**Cym. Warp One
'Cheltenham Nights'**
The parents of this
cymbidium were *Cym.*
Ngaire, a deep purple-red
from *Cym.* Rio Rita, and *Cym.*
Olive Street, a yellow-green
pendulous *Cym. devonianum*
hybrid. As with many second-
generation miniature hybrids,
the flowers are intermediate in
size between standards and
miniatures, as is the structure
of the plant. Similarly the
influence of *Cym. devonianum*
is diluted, so this hybrid can
be staked upright or allowed to
cascade.

Cymbidium hookerianum

Cym. hookerianum grows as an epiphyte at 5,000–7,000ft (1,500–2,000m) above sea level in the Himalayas in India, Nepal, and Tibet. It was introduced into cultivation by Thomas Lobb, who sent plants to Veitch's nursery, where it flowered for the first time in 1866, and where its clear green flowers created quite a stir. It is often seen today under the synonymous name of *Cym. grandiflorum*, and it is as *Cym. grandiflorum* that it appears in the hybrid lists as an important ancestor of so many modern cymbidiums. Although most growers prefer hybrids, *Cym. hookerianum* still deserves a place in a cymbidium collection. Hybrids cannot match the graceful charm of the arching spikes of up to twenty of the most intense green, spiky flowers, produced in spring by this species.

Cyperorchis elegans
Considered by some
authorities to be cymbidiums,
members of the genus
Cyperorchis grow in the same
areas of Asia as their near
relatives. Although they are
rarely seen in contemporary
collections, they are
reasonably easy to grow and
generally flower profusely.
This species is perhaps the
most common and has almost
no pseudobulbs, producing its
flower spikes from between
the leaves in late summer and
autumn. The numerous
yellow flowers do not open
fully, but hang like bells from
the spike.

Odontoglossum crispum
For many people this is the most beautiful of all orchids, and it has been thought of as such since its discovery in the Andes of Colombia, in 1841, by Hartweg. In the wild it was at one time quite common, but was reduced almost to the point of extinction, particularly during the frenzied trade collecting of the second half of the last century. It is particularly variable, and choice types changed hands for large sums of money. It grows epiphytically at 8,000–10,000ft (2,500–3,000m) above sea level, in cool Andean forests, and in cultivation is particularly intolerant of excess heat. Virtually all of the myriad hybrid odontoglossums, and related intergeneric hybrids, originate from this remarkable species.

Odontoglossum harryanum

This attractive species (opposite, top right) was first described in 1886, and named in honour of the nurseryman Harry Veitch. It is reported from Colombia and Peru, but it has been suggested that the true *Odm. harryanum* comes only from Colombia, the similar *Odm. wyattianum* being confined to Peru. If these are distinct species, then this illustration is the latter species, as are most of the

Odontoglossum maculatum

An attractive yellow and brown species from the montane forests of Mexico and Guatemala, *Odm. maculatum* (above) grows as an epiphyte, usually on species of oak. This species was introduced in 1824 and is easily grown in a shady, cool greenhouse, flowering in late spring or summer.

Odontoglossum pescatorei

For some authorities this species (left), sometimes known as *Odm. nobile*, is a form of *Odm. crispum*, but certainly from a hybridizer's point of view it is quite distinct. It comes from the same Andean forests as its near relative, and can be as challenging in cultivation. *Odm. pescatorei* produces a branched spike of white flowers with distinct pink markings, somewhat more numerous but smaller than those of *Odm. crispum*. It has collected numerous awards, and has contributed greatly to many hybrids.

Odontoglossum grande

Often called the clown orchid, referring to the structure at the centre of the flower, this species (right) is one of the most popular and reliable. It seems to thrive even in less than ideal conditions and is often successful as a house plant, producing its large yellow and brown flowers in late autumn. It was introduced by George Ure Skinner from Mexico, where it grows in montane forests, and was described by John Lindley in 1840. Now known correctly as *Rossioglossum grande*, it remains an all-time favourite.

Odm. Spring Jack
Most primary hybrids were
made in the early days of
orchid breeding, so it is
surprising to find that the
cross of _Odm. ure-skinneri_ and
Odm. harryanum has only
recently been made. As with
many primary hybrids, _Odm._
Spring Jack is vigorous and
easy to grow, and displays
identifiable characteristics of
each of its species parents.

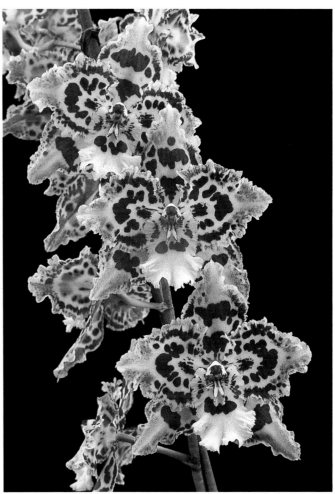

***Oda*. Nationwide**

Odontioda is an artificial
bigeneric hybrid genus
produced by crossing a
Cochlioda with an
Odontoglossum. Cochliodas
were originally used in
breeding to pass on their
bright red colour to the
offspring, but modern
odontiodas are many
generations removed from this
objective, and are produced in
many colours and shades. This
hybrid (above left) was made
by the English orchid firm of
Mansell and Hatcher, in
Leeds, by crossing *Oda*.
Carisette with *Oda*. Flocalo,
and was named after the
British television programme
on which it made its debut a
few years ago.

***Oda*. Tabor Heights**

This fine hybrid (above right)
was registered in 1980 by the
well-known English orchid
enthusiast, Eric Young. Its
parents were *Odm*. Jerespol
and *Oda*. Astargia. The
individual illustrated here is
typical of the cross, and indeed
has the maroon and white
colouring and markings of
many odontiodas. The flowers
are produced on long sprays,
which can be staked either
upright or gently arching.

Oda. **Harry Baldwin**

This hybrid was made in the hope of producing the elusive colour orange. As in all hybridizing the offspring vary, and these five plants (opposite) all came from one seed pod.

Oda. **Abigail 'Vaila'**

Much of the charm of this hybrid (above) derives from its parent, a pink form of the Mexican species *Odm. rossii*. It represents a little self-indulgence by the author. It is the only seedling I raised from the only hybrid I registered as an amateur. I named it after my daughter, Abigail, and my wife, Vaila, and it was given the Award of Merit by Britain's Royal Horitcultural Society in 1984.

Odtna. **Lulli 'Menuet'**

Odontonias are the result of a cross between an odontoglossum and a miltonia. Miltonias are used in breeding for their large size, and particularly for their large lip. *Odtna*. Lulli was made by the French orchid firm of Vacherot and Lecoufle, as were both its parents, and it was registered in 1942. Its parents were *Odontoglossum* Nabab, an almost pure bred *Odm. crispum*, and *Miltonia* Babiole. The cultivar 'Menuet' (right) was given an award by the American Orchid Society in 1975, and it is still a firm favourite.

Odcdm. Purbeck Gold

Odontocidiums are hybrids between odontoglossums and oncidiums. The yellow species *Oncidium tigrinum*, from Mexico, is often used, and in this case is crossed with the yellow *Odontoglossum* Gold Cup. The large lip of this oncidium is so characteristic and so dominant, that hybrids from it are quite similar to each other, almost regardless of which odontoglossum is used as the other parent. Odontocidiums are generally easier to grow than straight odontoglossums or odontiodas, and provide a reliable splash of bright yellow in a mixed collection.

**_Odcdm._ Ruhrgold
'Gaytarn'**
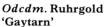
One of the best known of all
odontocidiums was _Odcdm._
Selsfield Gold, made in 1960
by David Sander. _Odcdm._
Ruhrgold (above left) is the
result of a cross between this
hybrid and the popular species
Odontoglossum bictoniense,
which, when it arrived in
1835, was the first of the genus
to be introduced to Europe.
Odcdm. Ruhrgold was made in
Germany by an amateur
orchid enthusiast, Kuno
Krieger, in 1984, and has
inherited its vigour from both
its parents, and its upright
spike habit from the species.
The rich orange lip colour
gives this cultivar a distinctive
character.

Vuyl. Cambria 'Plush'
Vuylstekearas are trigeneric
hybrids that include the
genera _Miltonia_, _Cochlioda_,
and _Odontoglossum_. _Vuyl._
Cambria was made by
Charlesworths in 1931 by
crossing _Vuyl._ Rudra with
Odm. Clonius. A First Class
Certificate was awarded to the
cultivar 'Plush' (above right)
by the British Royal
Horticultural Society in 1967
and by the American Orchid
Society in 1973. Over the
years it has been micro-
propagated by the thousands,
if not by the millions, and is
deservedly perhaps the best-
known of all orchid hybrids
throughout the world. It is
easy to grow and flower, and is
readily available.

Vuyl. Edna 'Stamperland'
During the early years of this
century the firm of
Charlesworths made two
primary intergeneric hybrids
using the bright red species
Cochlioda noezliana. These
were with *Odontoglossum
harryanum* to give *Odontioda*
Charlesworthii, and with
Miltonia vexillaria to give
Miltonioda Harwoodii. These
two were then crossed to
produce *Vuyl*. Edna. The
cultivar 'Stamperland' was
awarded a First Class
Certificate in England in 1929
and in America thirty years
later. Thanks to its robust
constitution it was still around
when micro-propagation came
along, and so, despite its age, it
is readily available today.

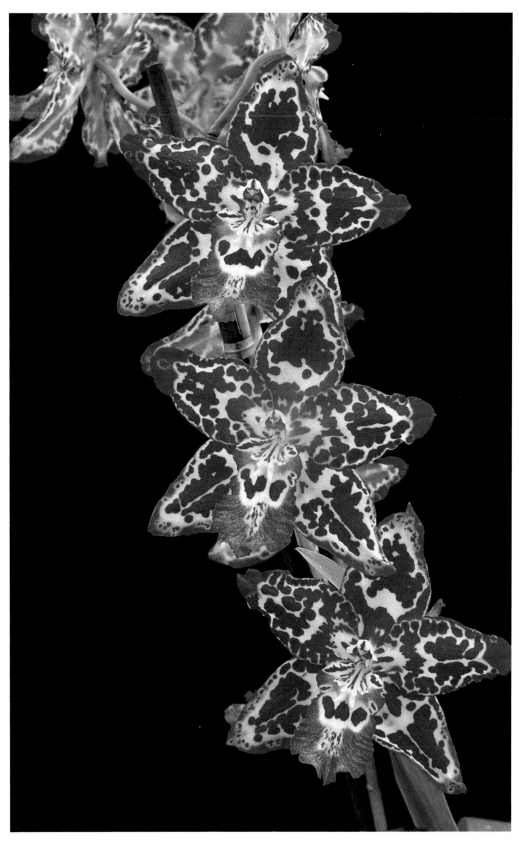

Wils. Tigersette

Wilsonaras are hybrids
involving members of three
genera, *Odontoglossum*,
Cochlioda, and *Oncidium*.
Straight odontoglossums and
odontiodas can be a challenge
to grow well, particularly in
warm summers, and the
introduction of oncidium
blood seems to ease this
problem. Many wilsonaras
originate in America, where
they are produced,
particularly in California, to
cope with a warm climate.
However, *Wilsonara*
Tigersette was a cross made in
England by Mansell and
Hatcher. The excellent shape
comes from one parent,
Odontioda Carisette, while its
tolerant constitution is
inherited from the other, the
Mexican species *Oncidium
tigrinum*.

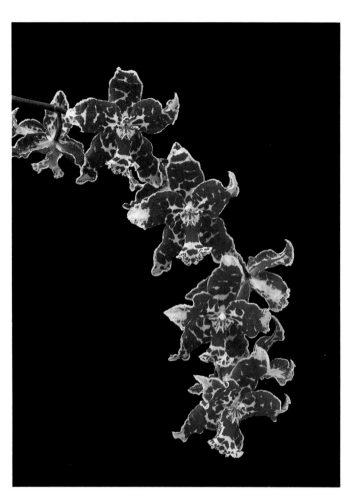

Sand. Rippon Tor 'Kitty Jay'

Sanderara is another hybrid genus involving three genera; it commemorates the great orchid name of Sander. The three genera involved are *Odontoglossum, Cochlioda,* and *Brassia.* This hybrid is a cross between *Sand.* Saint Helier and *Oda.* Queen Mary, and was made in England by the firm of Burnham Nurseries in 1985. The cultivar 'Kitty Jay' (above left) was given the Award of Merit by the British Royal Horticultural Society in 1988.

Mtssa. Penny Micklow 'Gaytarn'

Miltassias are hybrids between miltonias and brassias, in this case between *Brassia* Sunset Gold and *Miltonia* Goodale Moir, both of which are primary hybrids. *Miltassia* Penny Micklow (above right) was made in Florida in 1985, and clearly shows the characteristic spidery flowers of its brassia parent.

Paphiopedilum fairrieanum

In 1857 this charming species (right) created quite a stir when it was first shown by Mr Fairrie of Liverpool, after whom it was named by John Lindley. Very few were in cultivation and, as its origin remained a mystery, it soon became known as the lost orchid. In 1904 Frederick Sander offered a prize of £1,000, a great deal of money in those days, to anyone who could find it in the wild, and bring him a living specimen. The financial incentive worked, and in due course it was rediscovered and has remained a firm favourite

Paphiopedilum haynaldianum

Many species of this popular genus bear solitary flowers, but a few species generally from warmer areas of southeast Asia have several flowers on each stem. *Paphiopedilum haynaldianum* (above) was first collected by Wallis for the firm of Veitch & Sons in 1873, near Manila, in the Philippines. It is easy to grow in warm conditions, and produces its long-lasting flowers in winter and spring.

Paph. Shillianum

This fine old cross (left) was first made in 1899; it is one of many popular hybrids from *Paphiopedilum rothschildianum*. The other parent was *Paph.* Gowerianum, a primary hybrid between *Paph. curtisii* and *Paph. lawrenceanum*, made by Sander in 1893. *Paph. rothschildianum* itself is difficult and slow to grow, and needs the attention of an expert. Much easier are its hybrids, all of which make handsome additions to a warm-house collection.

Paph. micranthum 'Gaytarn'
It is easy to suppose that the world was thoroughly explored during the last few centuries, and that there are no surprises left. However, in just the last few years we have seen several spectacular new Paphiopedilums from southwest China, among them *Paphiopedilum micranthum*.

Paph. Bonnsure 'Bad Godesburg'
The large round standard hybrids are many generations removed from the wild species of Asia. The texture of the flowers is such that they appear to be made of wax or plastic, and they last, quite literally, for months. The parents of this hybrid were *Paph*. Enchantment and the famous *Paph*. Winston Churchill. The cultivar 'Bad Godesburg' (left) was recently given the Award of Merit by Britain's Royal Horticultural Society.

Paph. Vintage Harvest 'Bordeaux'

This magnificent green hybrid was made by the famous English orchid firm of Ratcliffes, a name that has for many years been synonymous with paphiopedilums. The cultivar 'Bordeaux' (right) was awarded a First Class Certificate, the highest possible award, by the British Royal Horticultural Society in 1987. It was also the winner of the 1987 George Moore Medal, an annual award for the best paphiopedilum shown during the year.

Phrag. Calurum

Phragmipediums are the Central and South American cousins of *Paphiopedilum*, a genus that is confined to India and southeast Asia. In the early days of orchid hybridizing John Seden worked at Veitch's nursery with John Dominy, the producer of the first orchid hybrid. His own first hybrid was *Phragmipedium* Sedenii, a cross between *Phrag. longifolium* and *Phrag. schlimii*, registered in 1873. Ten years later he flowered and registered *Phrag.* Calurum (left), a cross between his first hybrid and its parent, *Phrag. longifolium*. Phragmipediums are reasonably easy to grow in warm shady conditions. They produce several flowers per stem, usually in succession, with one fading as the next bud opens.

Paph. Gwenda Overett 'Midday Sun'

The species *Paph. primulinum* was discovered in Sumatra in 1972 and described as a new species in the following year. It has a succession of small, bright yellow flowers on an extending stem. The species was crossed with a conventional large hybrid paphiopedilum, *Paph.* Cherokee, by Beall, the American orchid company, and registered in 1979. It produces a number of flowers on each spike, intermediate in size between its parents. The delightful cultivar 'Midday Sun' (opposite, below) was given the Award of Merit of Britain's Royal Horticultural Society in 1988.

Phalaenopsis stuartiana
Orchids of the genus
Phalaenopsis, commonly called
moth orchids, are found in
India, throughout southeast
Asia, and in northern
Australia. *Phal. stuartiana*
(left) was originally found on
the island of Mindanao, one of
the Philippines, by William
Boxall, when he was collecting
orchids for the firm of Low &
Co in 1881. It was named after
Stuart Low. *Phal. stuartiana* is
one of a few species of
Phalaenopsis with attractive
silver-mottled leaves. It
should be grown in warm,
shady conditions.

Phalaenopsis schilleriana
When well grown this
attractive pink-flowered
species (right) can produce
large branched sprays with
several hundred flowers. It
comes from the Philippines,
and has mottled foliage. Many
large-flowered pink hybrids
have been produced from this
and other species.

65

Phal. Adorno

Phalaenopsis Adorno (left) is a hybrid between the small striped species *Phal. lindenii* and *Phal.* Intermedia, a natural hybrid between *Phal. aphrodite* and *Phal. equestris.* It was recently made in Hawaii. Large-flowered hybrids will always be popular, but there is a place for the rather more delicate miniature types, like this, which are produced from the smaller species.

Phal. Cashmore

Phalaenopsis Cashmore (above left) is the result of a cross between *Phal.* Party Dress, a medium-sized white of good shape, and a yellow cultivar of *Phal.* Barbara Moler, in this case 'Teignhills'. In recent years many phalaenopsis breeders have been trying to produce good, non-fading, yellow hybrids, to add to the traditional range of pinks and whites. *Phal.* Cashmore is a recent addition, produced by Keith Andrew Orchids.

Phal. Barbara Moler 'Teignhills'

Phalaenopsis Barbara Moler was produced in the United States in 1971, and has been an important parent for many phalaenopsis breeders. The cross produced quite variable offspring, some white with pink spots, and some in varying shades of yellow. The cultivar 'Teignhills' (above right) is particularly good, and has produced many fine yellow offspring over the years.

Phal. **Cashmore**

This hybrid (above) is the result of a cross using *Phal.* Barbara Moler 'Plush', a white and pink cultivar. The results are still called *Phal.* Cashmore, in accordance with the rules of hybrid registration, although this cross produced no yellow offspring. We must take care when purchasing any orchids not in flower to understand what the names on the label mean. If, as in this case, the plant has the hybrid name Cashmore, but no cultivar name to identify it as an individual, then it could be any individual produced from any *Phal.* Party Dress (most were pink, only one was white) with any *Phal.* Barbara Moler (some were pink, some pale yellow, and a few deep yellow).

Phal. Marquis of Bath

Phalaenopsis Marquis of Bath (opposite, below left) is one of many standard whites that have been produced in recent years. The modern requirements are for large, flat, round flowers on long sprays. Most standard white hybrids have been produced by many generations of selective breeding from just two original species, *Phal. aphrodite* and *Phal. amabilis*. The parents of this hybrid are *Phal.* Frank Gottburg and *Phal.* Temple Cloud, one bred in the United States and the other in England.

Phal. Lippetor

Perhaps the single most significant contribution to phalaenopsis breeding during the last twenty years or so has been made in Germany, by Fritz Hark, who has produced an impressive series of large pinks. This hybrid (above) is a cross between two of his fine pinks, *Phal.* Lipperose and *Phal.* Lippeglut.

Phal. Liseron

For some time the famous French firm of Vacherot and Lecoufle have been breeding spotted *Phalaenopsis* orchids, and this hybrid (left) is the latest in a long line. This particular pattern of spotting is characteristic of hybrids from the species *Phal. stuartiana*, although *Phal.* Liseron represents many further generations of progress.

Phal. Dorset Bride

Candy stripes in phalaenopsis are produced by selective use of two small-flowered species, *Phal. equestris* and *Phal. lindenii*, combined with large white hybrids. Deep red lips also come from *Phal. equestris*. *Phal.* Dorset Bride (above) is a fine example of the combination of good size and shape with stripes and a red lip.

C. Mary Jane Proebstle
This fine white hybrid (above) was registered in the United States in 1960. The parents were the famous white *C.* Bob Betts and the natural hybrid *C.* Obrieniana. Cattleyas, and hybrids involving related genera, are easily grown in intermediate conditions with good light. They readily produce their flamboyant flowers, usually in winter, and many are successfully grown on windowsills.

Lc. Gaillard 'Noel'
For many people a large mauve cattleya such as this represents their idea of a typical orchid. In fact this (right) is a *Laeliocattleya*, a bigeneric hybrid between a *Cattleya* and a *Laelia*; it was produced in France and registered in 1945.

_Lc_. Stradivarius 'Tiede'
This hybrid (left) was
produced in 1974 by Vacherot
and Lecoufle from a crossing
of two other laeliocattleyas,
one _Lc_. Dusky Maid from the
United States and the other,
_Lc_. Roitelet, from France. The
colour is a vibrant salmon
pink, which makes a welcome
addition to the standard
colours of this group.

_Lc_. Culminant 'La Tuilerie'
This French hybrid (left) was
bred from _Lc_. Gaillard in
1957. Much orchid breeding
over the years has been
directed to producing larger,
rounder, and flatter flowers,
and this principle has been
applied to many genera. These
qualities are seen in this fine
hybrid, with the wide petals
completely filling the gaps
between the sepals to produce
a near-perfect shape.

Lc. (Grodske's Gold × C. David Sweet)
This very new hybrid has yet to be named and registered, so it is only known at present by the names of its parents. *Lc.* Grodske's Gold is a small intense yellow hybrid bred from *Laelia flava*, a species from Brazil. Not all hybrids are large, round, and flat, and for many enthusiasts the open shapes are more natural and more attractive.

Milt. vexillaria 'Burnham'
The genus *Miltonia* is now
strictly confined to the group
of orchids from Brazil. The
large-flowered pansy orchids
have been reclassified, so this
species should correctly be
called *Miltoniopsis vexillaria*.
The new genus consists of five
species that grow in the
mountain forests of Costa
Rica, Panama, Venezuela,
Colombia, and Ecuador. They
have been used extensively by
breeders to produce hybrids
that are still commonly called
miltonias, under which name
they remain for hybrid
registration purposes. The
cultivar 'Burnham' (left) is a
particularly fine pink form of
what is usually a white or pale
pink species.

Milt. Beethoven 'Plush'
Miltonia Beethoven is a cross
between two famous parents,
Milt. Lycaena and *Milt*. Mrs
J. B. Crum, a fine deep red and
itself a hybrid from *Milt*.
Lycaena. The cultivar 'Plush'
(right) is a particularly well-
defined example of what is
known as a waterfall miltonia.
The effect of a waterfall on the
lip is inherited in part from the
rare species *Milt. phalaenopsis*.

Milt. Lorene
This hybrid (right) has a well-marked lip with a well-defined mask. It is an American hybrid registered in 1984 from a crossing of *Milt*. Paula Jean and *Milt*. Andrea Baker. Miltonias are reasonably easy to grow in an intermediate greenhouse or even in a warm room. They dislike cold or dry conditions.

Milt. Emotion 'Burnham'
This old favourite (right) was made in France in 1945 from a crossing of *Milt*. Emoi with *Milt*. Nyasa, and has been used extensively as a parent of further generations. The distinctive purple eyes at the base of the petals are characteristic of the Colombian species *Milt*. *roezlii*, from which they are inherited. Like most miltonias, this hybrid is pleasantly scented.

Lyc. Auburn 'Ethereal'

Lycaste Auburn has been one of the outstanding hybrid lycastes of all time. It was registered over thirty years ago from a cross between the primary hybrid, *Lyc.* Balliae (*Lyc. macrophylla* × *Lyc. skinneri*) and *Lyc.* Sunrise. Unlike most popular orchids, lycastes are deciduous, often flowering when the pseudobulbs are leafless. They make good companions for cymbidiums, enjoying much the same cool-greenhouse conditions, with perhaps a little more shade in summer. The long-lasting flowers are unfortunately very easily bruised, leaving unsightly brown marks, so care must be taken when moving them. For this reason they are a challenge to exhibit.

Lyc. Jason

Lycaste Jason (left) is a primary hybrid between *Lyc. macrobulbon* and *Lyc. lasioglossa*, and was made in 1964 by Wyld Court Orchids, an English orchid firm that has always been synonymous with lycaste breeding. With most popular orchids it is the lip that dominates the flower, with the petals second. With lycastes it is sepals first and petals second, with a relatively small lip relegated to third place. Many of the species have a strong spicy perfume, and this is sometimes passed on to the hybrids.

Disa Diores 'Inca Queen'

Disas originate in South Africa where they grow as terrestrials. This hybrid is principally derived from the spectacular red species *Disa uniflora*, which is often found growing alongside streams with its roots in water. The species have always had the reputation of being very difficult to grow, but the hybrids appear to be somewhat more tolerant. *Disa* Diores was originally raised by Veitch, in 1898, from a crossing of *Disa uniflora* with *Disa* Veitchii, itself a hybrid from *Disa uniflora*. The cultivar 'Inca Queen' (left) was from a recent remake of the cross raised in England, and was one of several that earned the Award of Merit from Britain's Royal Horticultural Society.

Disa hybrids

Four different cultivars of the red hybrid *Disa* Diores are shown (right), together with the yellow *Disa* Kewensis 'Milkmaid'. *Disa* Kewensis is a primary hybrid between the red *Disa uniflora* and *Disa tripetaloides*, a small multi-flowered white species. It was originally raised at Kew in 1893 and is usually pink. The plant shown is from a batch raised recently using *Disa tripetaloides* ssp. *aurata*, a yellow sub-species. Disa flowers may not immediately look like orchids, but closer examination reveals three dominant sepals with two small petals clutching the upright column and a tiny ribbon-like lip.

Zyg. Blackii 'Negus'

Zygopetalum Blackii is a cross
made, in 1914, by the old
orchid firm of Black & Flory,
between *Zyg.* Perrenoudii and
the species *Zyg. crinitum.* It is
a tribute to the vigour of
zygopetalum hybrids that so
many of the best are still
around from so long ago and
that they are still popular.
Flowers are produced in late
autumn, and have the
delightful perfume of
hyacinths. The lips of many
zygopetalums are as near to
the elusive blue as we
ordinarily see in orchid
collections, except perhaps in
some vandas.

Pptm. **Mathina**

Zygopetalums are particularly prone to apomixis, an unusual natural process by which seed is produced when the stigma is stimulated by foreign pollen. The offspring are identical to the mother plant, as no fertilization takes place, but the process has confused hybridizers into believing that they have succeeded with some most unusual crosses. When the cross of *Zygopetalum mackayi* with *Promenaea xanthina* was first reported in 1976 there was much suspicion that the offspring would all turn out to be *Z. mackayi*. However, this remarkable hybrid (left) is clearly a propetalum, with the flower shape and plant growth of a zygopetalum and the yellow colour of a promenaea.

Cirr. **Elizabeth Ann 'Bucklebury'**

Cirrhopetalum is a genus of thirty or so species found in Africa, Asia, and some Pacific Islands, and it is related to the enormous genus *Bulbophyllum*. They should be grown in baskets rather than pots, as the plants have a rather scrambling habit. This curious primary hybrid (left) was raised from a cross between *Cirr. longissima* and *Cirr. rothschildianum*. It was given an Award of Merit by the British Royal Horticultural Society and, thanks to micro-propagation, is now generally available.

Dendrobium thyrsiflorum
This easily grown cool-house species is sometimes known as *Dendrobium densiflorum* var. *albo-lutea*. The normal form of *Den. densiflorum* has all-yellow flowers. This group of *Dendrobium* species come from India, Burma, and Nepal, where they grow in the foothills of the Himalayas. The Indian dendrobiums generally need a cool dry rest in winter in order to flower well in spring.

***Den*. Thwaitesiae 'Veitch'**
This early dendrobium hybrid (left) was registered in 1903, and the cultivar 'Veitch' was awarded a First Class Certificate by the British Royal Horticultural Society in the following year. It is a semi-deciduous hybrid and is easy to grow, requiring a cool dry and light rest in the winter to flower well in the spring. It is a testament to its toughness that it is still around and still available.

Dendrobium aphyllum
The correct name for this species (above) is *Den. aphyllum*, but it is commonly grown as *Den. pierardii*. Its long canes are pendulous, so it is best grown on bark, or in a basket, rather than in a pot. The canes are deciduous and must be ripened with a cool, dry, and light winter to ensure that they flower well in the spring. New canes then grow during the summer, to flower the following spring.

***Den.* Hot Pulany 'Kibi'**
For many years the name of
Yamamoto has been
synonymous with the breeding
of the semi-deciduous group
of dendrobiums. This recent
hybrid is very much like a
superior *Den. nobile.*
Yamamoto hybrids are
available in a wide range of
colours, are easy to grow, and
flower profusely in the spring.

Den. Ella Victoria Leaney
This primary hybrid (below) was raised in Australia from a crossing of two native Australian species, *Den. kingianum* and *Den. ruppianum*. *Den. kingianum* has been a favourite for many years because it is easy to grow and to flower in cool conditions. In recent years several hybrids have been made using the Australian dendrobiums. They are generally very easy plants, producing a profusion of flowers in spring.

Den. (Ekapol × Doreen)
This recent hybrid has yet to be named and registered. It belongs to the warm-growing group of tropical evergreen dendrobiums. In this group the flower spikes are produced from the end of the canes, and the flowers are very long lasting, either on the plant or cut. This particular hybrid (right) was bred, along with many others, in southeast Asia, where dendrobiums of this type are grown in large numbers for the international cut-flower trade.

Vanda Rothschildiana

If warm-house conditions can be provided, then *Vanda* Rothschildiana (left) is a must, not least because it is one of the few blue orchids. It is a hybrid between the spectacular *V. sanderiana* and the pale blue species *V. coerulea* and was first made in France in 1931. Vandas require warm, moist, and light conditions to flower well, and they are often grown in baskets so that their roots can hang in the air.

Vanda Kasem's Delight

Many hybrids have been made from *V. sanderiana* and *V.* Rothschildiana, particularly in southeast Asia, where they form the basis of a large cut-flower industry. Singapore and Bangkok are the centres of this rural-based industry, and many thousands of cut orchid spikes are exported every day. This hybrid (above), which was made in Thailand in 1978, has been used extensively as a parent of other hybrids.

Rhrds. Thai Noi

In Asia there are many genera of orchids, related to vandas, that require warm and light conditions to thrive. They are a challenge to grow well in areas that have dull cold winters and, sadly, they are rarely seen. Very many fine hybrids and many unusual intergeneric hybrids have, however, been made in warmer climates, where they form the basis of orchid cultivation and trade, particularly in southeast Asia. This _Rhynchorides_ (below) is just such an unusual hybrid, made in Thailand in 1973 from a cross of _Aërides flabellata_ and _Rhynchostylis coelestis_.

Vanda Kasem's Delight

The tessellated markings, which are characteristic of hybrids from _V. coerulea_, are clearly seen in this pink hybrid (right), photographed with the sun shining through the petals and sepals. Vanda flowers are long lasting either on the plant or cut. Unlike most popular orchids these flowers do not rely on the lip to contribute to their beauty.

Masdevallia strobelii
The genus *Masdevallia* consists of numerous species from Central and South America. They are particularly abundant in the cool cloud forests on the eastern slopes of the Andes, where they grow as epiphytes. The sepals of the flowers are fused to form a tube, often with three tails, which encloses the small petals and lip. Masdevallias should be grown in a cool, moist, and shady spot. They have no pseudobulbs, so need constant moisture, and they particularly dislike warm and dry conditions. *Masd. strobelli* (above) is an attractive, free-flowering species from Ecuador.

Masd. Prince Charming

Masdevallias have enjoyed something of a revival in recent times, having been a favourite genus during the last century. The Victorian era saw forty-six hybrid masdevallias registered, but since then there has been only one in the 1960s, four in the 1970s and eleven so far in the 1980s. This revival has been led by hybridizers in the United States. One such recent hybrid is *Masd*. Prince Charming (left), a primary hybrid between *Masd. angulata* and the large red species *Masd. veitchiana*. It was made in 1979 in California.

Pleurothallis trifida

The genus *Pleurothallis* is one of the largest of orchid genera, with perhaps as many as fifteen hundred species confined to Central and South America. The vast majority are small plants, some quite minute; they are most abundant in the cool moist montane forests of the Andes. These intriguing orchids (below), and many other miniature genera, reveal their subtle beauty only under the magnification of a hand lens. Those enthusiasts who grade orchids by their flamboyance and measure the beauty of their flowers in inches, often refer disparagingly to these gems of nature as 'botanicals'.

Dryadella zebrina

The genus *Dryadella* is often still included in the closely related genus *Masdevallia*. These miniatures come from Brazil, and are affectionately known as partridge-in-the-grass orchids. *Dryadella zebrina* (right) is the most common species in cultivation.

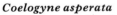

Coelogyne asperata

There are over a hundred
species in the genus *Coelogyne*,
found throughout southeast
Asia. In cultivation they are
divided into two groups, those
from the highlands of India,
Burma, and Malaya, which
grow well in a cool-house, and
those from the lowlands of
southeast Asia, which require
warm conditions. *Coelogyne
asperata* (above left), a large
plant from Malaysia, Sumatra,
and New Guinea, requires
warmth. The cream flowers
are scented and are produced
in spring.

Coelogyne ochracea

Perhaps this species (above
right) should correctly be
known as *Coel. nitida*, but it
has been familiar to
generations of orchid growers
under this name. It soon
grows into a large plant, when
a profusion of flowers are
reliably produced in late
spring. An all-time favourite,
it has a delightful and
distinctive perfume.

Coelogyne cristata
This easily grown cool-house species is one of the best known, and best loved, of all orchids. It is an orchid that is often grown successfully as a house plant by non-specialists. *Coelogyne cristata* comes from the eastern end of the Himalayas. The clear white flowers are produced in spring, and in India are often used for decoration at weddings.

Aërangis rhodosticta

Members of the genus *Aërangis* are confined to tropical Africa and Madagascar where they grow as epiphytes. *A. rhodosticta* has always been a firm favourite with orchid growers, and thrives on a piece of bark in a shady spot in the warm house. Good well grown plants may produce several long racemes, each bearing as many as twenty-five long lasting flowers.

Oncidium concolor
For such a small plant *Oncidium concolor* (left) produces relatively large flowers. Like many oncidiums, it is best grown on a piece of bark, or in a basket. The species is easy to grow and is readily available. It originates in the Organ Mountains of Brazil.

Maxillaria lepidota
This (right) is one of upward of three hundred species in this genus, many of them rarely seen in orchid collections. They are related to the genus *Lycaste*, and are found throughout tropical and sub-tropical America, where they grow as epiphytes. Maxillarias are generally easy to grow and to flower, and are well worth including in a collection for their particularly interesting range of spicy scents.

Maxillaria tenuifolia

This species is an easily grown favourite producing flowers that are said to smell of coconut. It comes from Central America, from Mexico to Costa Rica, where it grows epiphytically in rain forests. *Max. tenuifolia* (left) produces pseudobulbs that are spaced out along an ascending rhizome. This growth habit makes for easier cultivation on a slab of bark, to which extensions can be added as the plant grows.

Encyclia cochleata

Often still known as *Epidendrum cochleatum*, this species (right) from Central America was one of the first epiphytes to be grown successfully in Europe. The flowers are carried with the deep purple lip uppermost and the twisted greenish petals and sepals hanging down. They open in succession on a spike that can keep flowering into its second year, by which time the next year's growth may also be in flower. If grown well there is therefore no reason why this orchid should not have some flowers all the time.

Stanhopea oculata

There are about twenty-five species of *Stanhopea* (left) widely distributed in the American tropics, where they grow as epiphytes. They have strange and fascinating flowers that always arouse great curiosity. They are produced in summer and last for only a few days, but they have the most intense and intoxicating perfume. Stanhopeas are easy plants in cultivation, but must be grown in wire or wooden slatted baskets as the flower spikes grow vertically downward from the base of the pseudobulbs.

Anoectochilus roxburghii

Unlike most orchids, which have relatively uninteresting foliage, the jewel orchids are grown for their remarkably patterned leaves. There are several genera, coming from Asia, where they grow in the deep shade of the forest floor. They are not easy plants to grow well, needing evenly warm, shady, humid, and moist conditions. When they are well grown they produce upright spikes of white flowers. *Anoectochilus roxburghii* (above) comes from northern India and is one of the most attractive species.

Neofinetia falcata

The genus *Neofinetia* consists of this single species (above), which is found in Korea and Japan, where selected cultivars with variegated foliage are highly prized. It is related to vandas, and produces its white flowers from between the leaves. The flowers have a long hollow spur projecting backward from the base of the lip, an indication that it is probably pollinated by a butterfly or a moth.

Laelia gouldiana
This Mexican species (above),
together with *L. autumnalis*
and *L. anceps*, are favourite
autumn-flowering orchids for
cool conditions. The Mexican
laelias like a cool, dry and light
rest in winter, after they have
flowered. They are readily
available and are easy and
rewarding orchids for the
beginner.

Laelia milleri
Unlike most members of the
genus *Laelia*, this species
(left) has quite small flowers.
It has been used in breeding
with *L. harpophylla* and *L.
cinnabarina*, to introduce its
intense orange colour into
laeliocattleyas. These species
come from Brazil and are
moderately easy to grow in
intermediate conditions.

Pleione formosana
Now regarded as a variety of
P. bulbocodioides by botanists,
this deciduous species is found
in Tibet, China, and Formosa
where it grows up to 9,000ft
(2,750m) above sea level. It
should be grown in very cool
conditions, even in a cold
frame, and is often included in
alpine collections. It makes
a fine windowsill plant,
particularly if a number of
bulbs are planted together.

Galeandra baueri
Named by John Lindley after
the outstanding botanical
artist Francis Bauer,
Galeandra baueri is a curious
rather than beautiful orchid
from Central and South
America. Galeandras have
elongated pseudobulbs with
leaves arranged along their
length. The flower spikes are
produced from the apex of the
pseudobulbs.

Rhynchostylis gigantea
The genus consists of four species from the tropics of southeast Asia. They are related to the strap-leaved vandas, which they resemble in plant structure. The pendulous flower spikes are produced from between the leaves. This fragrant species comes from Thailand and should be grown along with vandas in warm conditions. The plant illustrated is a particularly fine example of this variable species.

Ada aurantiaca
This species comes from the
cool forests of the Andes of
Colombia and Ecuador, where
it grows alongside many of its
relatives, the odontoglossums.
The attractive bright orange
flowers do not open fully but
are bell-shaped and are
produced in spring. In recent
years this species has been
raised from seed, and it is now
readily available.

Comparettia macroplectron
These delightful relatives of the oncidiums come from the Andes of South America. Although they are not often seen in cultivation they deserve a place in the intermediate house for their delicate flowers. *C. macroplectron* (left) blooms in summer producing 12–15in (30–38cm) flower spikes, each with five to ten relatively large pink flowers.

Dendrochilum glumaceum
Although the individual flowers of this species, and indeed of most other members of the genus, are quite small they are produced in long racemes and have a most delightful perfume. *D. glumaceum* (right) is easy to grow in cool or intermediate conditions and flowers freely in the spring.

Calanthe vestita

The genus *Calanthe* is divided
into two groups, one evergreen
and one deciduous. *Calanthe
vestita* (opposite) is the most
familiar member of the latter
section; it is widespread in
southeast Asia. The long
flower spikes are produced in
winter from the bare
pseudobulbs. Several hybrids
were made in Victorian times
when they were popular as cut
flowers for Christmas.

Restrepia xanthophthalma

These small orchids are
related to the genus
Pleurothallis, and are
sometimes included with
them. There are about thirty
species, which grow as
epiphytes in cool moist
mountain conditions, from
Mexico to Argentina. The
species are quite similar and
all are small curiosities well
worth a place in a mixed
collection.

Ophrys sphegodes

This species (right and far right) is one of a number of members of the genus, common in the southern half of Europe from France through Italy, Greece, and the Balkans to the Crimea, that have flowers resembling insects. It is known in England as the early spider orchid and is confined to a few sites in Kent and Dorset, where it flowers in April. Here (far right) we see it at the very northern point of its distribution, flowering on the sea cliffs of the southern tip of Dorset.

Dactylorhiza fuchsii
This (above left) is the
common spotted orchid which
was, at one time, widespread
throughout Britain and
western and central Europe.
Although the spread of
modern agricultural methods
has depleted the population of
all orchids, this species still
survives, sometimes in
reasonable numbers,
particularly on the alkaline
soils of southern England –
there are still some areas at the
margins of woods, and on
unimproved downland, where
it grows in sufficient numbers
to create a mauve haze in early
summer.

Neottia nidus-avis
Commonly known as the
bird's nest orchid because of
its tangle of roots, this species
(above right) is found
throughout Europe. It grows
in the leaf litter in the deep
shade of woods, often beech or
pine, and produces its curious
flowers in early summer. This
species is a saprophyte – that
is, it lives off the dead remains
of other organisms, in this case
leaves. It has no chlorophyll,
gaining its nutrients not from
photosynthesis but entirely via
the mycorrhizal fungus in its
roots. It can therefore grow in
very dark conditions.

6

CULTURE

One of the myths about orchids is that they are difficult to cultivate. Early importations were grown, or rather were slowly killed, in entirely inappropriate conditions, so they came to be regarded as difficult, and still that reputation persists. Of course there are some that are difficult and indeed some that are near-impossible; it would be surprising with such a large family if this were not the case, but very many are quite easy. It is probable that a week or two of drought, or wet, or cold would see the end of many house plants, but not so with many orchids. Indeed it is very difficult to kill an orchid plant outright, and particularly difficult to do so by neglect. However, it is also fair to say that it is not easy to grow orchids to perfection, and most of us, whilst striving to improve, settle for something in between.

A greenhouse is not the only place to grow orchids. If care is taken to choose appropriate types, orchids can be successfully grown as house plants, on windowsills, or in growing cases, or even under artificial lights in a basement. So long as the plant receives the correct level of warmth, moisture, food, humidity, and light, in the correct seasons, then it cares little where it is housed. (However, it may matter to us if, for instance, the correct level of humidity for our orchids causes the lounge wallpaper to turn green and peel off.)

Greenhouse Culture

Orchids are not so different that the greenhouse must be devoted to them alone. Benjamin Williams wrote in *The Orchid Growers' Manual* at the end of the last century that 'It is not absolutely necessary to build a house for the cultivation of Orchids, for many people grow them most luxuriantly in ... houses principally devoted to flowering and ornamental-leaved plants.' This advice is still good, although it does depend on the other functions that the greenhouse may be called upon to perform. If an existing structure is used for seed raising in spring, tomatoes in summer, chrysanthemums in autumn, and assorted bicycles and lawnmowers during the winter, then there will have to be a rethink. There are many plants that will grow with orchids, but to approach a mixed collection from the other direction, by adding a few orchids to whatever is already being grown, may well make life difficult for the orchids. However, many people start this way, and soon find that the geraniums and fuchsias are ousted by an expanding orchid collection.

There are many different styles of greenhouse available, and orchids are grown successfully in them all. There is not necessarily an ideal, but there is an optimum, so let us assume a start from scratch, and generalize about that optimum. The size should not be less than 100 sq ft (9m²) as it is very difficult to maintain even conditions in small structures. They are very quickly heated by the sun, and as temperatures rise we have to open the windows. Out goes the beautiful moist atmosphere to be replaced by dry and, in winter, cold air. Orchids dislike these violent fluctuations in conditions, and so the larger the greenhouse, the slower are the changes and the easier it is to manage.

The greenhouse should be as near square as

possible. Long, narrow houses have proportionally larger surface areas, and so cost more to heat per square foot. Given a width of 15–18ft (4.5–5.5m), then, providing there is sufficient headroom, side and centre staging with two paths can be the layout. This is absolutely ideal, as tall plants can then grow on the central staging, under the ridge.

Many modern greenhouses are sold with glass to the ground, which is economical to manufacture. It is a good design for tomatoes and the like, but expensive to heat. Most orchids will be grown in pots on some form of staging, so the provision of light at ground level is unnecessary. An ideal would be the traditional design with solid walls to staging height, or a little above.

Siting is also important. An open aspect should be chosen, away from overhanging trees, where low winter light from the south is available. It should be near the house so that services (water, electricity, etc) can be provided, and it should be sheltered from cold winds from the north and east. This is an ideal, and some compromise may have to be made, but the provision of maximum winter light is perhaps the most important. Most orchids grow naturally in situations of more even day length than we have further north, and, while most welcome the extra day length in summer, many dislike the short, dull days of winter.

The largest single overhead in growing orchids is the cost of heating, so an efficient and well-controlled system is essential. There are many different ways to provide heat, and each will have its followers, so recommendations are inevitably personal. Whatever system is chosen, though, the provision of an accurate and reliable thermostat is most important, not only to maintain the correct temperature for the plants, but because it will save on heating costs. Each extra 1°C can increase heating costs by 10 to 20 per cent! The very best types provide for different day and night temperatures, controlled by a light sensor.

Again in the pursuit of economy, many orchid growers use some form of double glazing. Various materials, including rigid plastic, double-skinned bubble polythene and single thickness polythene are suitable. Whichever material is used it should be tightly fixed to exclude all draughts, and to provide a pocket of still air to act as the insulator. It is a good idea to empty the greenhouse completely in autumn and to tidy and disinfect the inside. The glass should be cleaned both inside and out, and if new lining is required it should be installed at this stage. The plants can then be individually cleaned and tidied and returned one by one to their quarters ready for the winter.

Orchid houses will require some form of shading. There are many options available, but the important factor to bear in mind is that shading is required to control summer temperatures, particularly leaf temperatures, and not to reduce the light level. Light is food to the plants, and they can use more than we might imagine, but with light comes heat, particularly behind glass, and it is the heat that does the damage. For this reason the best shading system is one that can be adjusted or removed on dull days. Shading on the inside of the greenhouse will exclude just as much light as it would were it on the outside, but it is next to useless because it will do nothing to control the heat. The object of the exercise is to stop the rays of the sun before they reach the glass, so the best system by far is shading on the outside, with an air gap of several inches between the glass and the shading material.

Most amateur greenhouses are supplied with insufficient ventilation. The ideal is for roof vents alternately on either side of the ridge, and running the whole length of the house. They can then be opened on the opposite side from the wind to give draught-free ventilation. Ventilation at staging level should not be used, but some means of admitting fresh air at ground level is desirable. Orchids need fresh air, but too much ventilation in winter can lead to cold draughts, which they certainly do not like. If the summer shading system is not efficient there is a tendency to resort to excessive ventilation to keep the greenhouse temperature down. The result is that it is impossible then to keep the humidity high enough, and the orchids suffer.

Some movement of air inside the greenhouse seems to be beneficial, particularly in winter when little ventilation is possible. Electric fans are available, and one mounted in the ridge pointing diagonally downwards will move the warmer air back down towards the floor. This helps to prevent pockets of cold stagnant air in odd corners. Many growers keep their fan running continuously.

Much of the above could well apply to a variety of tropical plants, save perhaps that cacti would dislike the level of shading, but it is with their requirements for controlled humidity that orchids differ. Most are, after all, epiphytes and for them the atmosphere is crucial. It is for this reason more than any other that care must be taken when recommending that orchids are easy, and can be grown with other plants. Humidity more than anything else seems to cause problems for beginners; problems usually of understanding.

Humidity is a measure of the amount of water vapour in the air. It could most simply be expressed in terms of volume of liquid water, say in cubic centimetres, held in a volume of air, say a cubic metre. This may well be accurate, and easily understood, but humidity is not measured in this straightforward way, because such a figure would have little use. Warm air can hold very much more water vapour than cold air and as the temperature rises we, and our plants, sense that the humidity is falling, even though it is not falling in absolute terms. Similarly, as the temperature drops in the evening we sense that the humidity is rising, and dew may result if the temperature drops to a point where the air can no longer hold the humidity of the day. What living things react to, plants and people alike, is not absolute humidity, but relative humidity, and that is how it is measured. Relative humidity is expressed as a percentage of the maximum capacity of the air at that particular temperature. If the temperature rises the air's capacity increases, so if no more water vapour is introduced the relative humidity falls and the air feels drier. As the temperature drops the relative humidity rises, eventually to 100 per cent (saturation) and at that temperature, called the dew point, moisture is precipitated out as dew on the ground, or as clouds in the atmosphere.

The traditional method of maintaining humidity in the greenhouse is by the process of damping down. This involves splashing water on the floor and under the staging, usually from a hose pipe. Foliage plants under the staging will help to maintain humidity, but may also provide a home for slugs and other pests. Electric humidifiers are available and

can be automated via a humidistat. As with all automatic greenhouse systems they are particularly useful for orchid growers who have to be away from their collections for significant periods.

As with all things in nature, there must be a balance. Experienced orchid growers can sense this balance and speak of a buoyant greenhouse atmosphere, claiming to have a nose for the right conditions. As a beginner this is of little help. What is meant is a balance of warmth, light, and fresh, humid air, and with experience this sense will come.

Indoor Culture

In recent times more and more orchids are grown indoors, and great strides in their cultivation have been made. Growing plants indoors is not a totally new development. Victorian parlours often housed an aspidistra or a palm, which survived the low light levels. Also common and very popular were magnificent maidenhair ferns, which we now grow well with orchids in our greenhouses, but which were then grown indoors. The Victorians were also successful with some orchids, lycastes in particular, which we would certainly not now recommend as ideal for indoor culture. If we examine why these changes should have occurred, we will see the clues to successful indoor culture of not only orchids, but also of many other plants.

Victorian houses were quite dark places, and plants were placed near windows. Popular plants then, as now, were plants whose natural habitat was shady forests, so bright light was not necessary. Lace or net curtains were fashionable for the privacy which they provided, and were ideal shading from scorching sun. Before central heating and modern building methods the houses were evenly cool and damp. The combination of these conditions provided an ideal environment for the ferns and the lycastes, and for other plants from cool forests. Modern conditions differ most significantly in the dry atmosphere and the higher temperatures provided by modern building methods and central heating. Many cool-growing ferns, particularly the many varieties of maidenhair fern, do not like this warm dry atmosphere, and the kinds of plants that are now successfully grown indoors, including orchids, originate from tropical forests. Our houses are warm enough and, short of direct summer sun scorching the leaves, it is possible to find a place with sufficient natural light, but providing humidity is now the major problem. The success of any plant from a tropical forest is likely to depend most on its ability to tolerate levels of humidity far below its ideal.

Providing that these limitations are borne in mind, and efforts are made to compensate for the disadvantages, then a surprisingly large range of orchids can be grown indoors.

Optimum light levels are provided on east- or west-facing windowsills, but never too near the glass and never between the glass and closed curtains. Local humidity can be provided by standing the pots on wet gravel in trays, but never so that the pot is actually in the water. All indoor plants benefit from being grown together in groups, because it is then possible to create a humid microclimate amongst them, particularly if the collection includes some foliage houseplants. This humid air amongst the foliage is an ideal habitat for the aerial roots of orchids.

An alternative is an orchid case or indoor greenhouse. These modern equivalents of the Wardian case provide an ideal humid atmosphere for orchids and are available in a variety of shapes and finishes, often designed as attractive pieces of display furniture. Thermostatic heating and automatic lights are built in.

Some enthusiasts have utilized spare space such as a basement to house their collections. These areas may be naturally humid and well insulated from rapid fluctuations of temperature. Certainly, in terms of energy costs, it is far cheaper to provide artificial light than heat, and particularly in cold parts of North America, basement growing under lights is popular.

There are several interesting temperate terrestrial orchids from Europe, Asia, and North America that can be successfully cultivated in an unheated alpine house, in a cold frame, or in the garden. They are most likely to be found in the catalogues of ordinary nurserymen or of alpine-plant specialists. Some orchids, such as the popular *Pleione* species from the Himalayas, span the distinction between alpines and specialist orchids, and are grown in Britain as indoor plants, in cool greenhouses, in alpine houses, in cold frames, and in sheltered and dry areas in the open garden.

Temperature

In the early days of orchid growing many thousands of tropical orchids were killed because it was supposed that they all came from hot, steamy jungles, so they were placed in the hot houses of the day. It is surprising how many people still associate orchids with such extreme climates, as if such exotic flowers could not possibly grow in pleasantly cool mountain forests. As information was passed on from collectors, and understanding increased, it became apparent that there were a wide variety of different climates in the tropics, not least as a result of the effects of altitude. At the height of the Victorian craze for orchids the nurseries, and the large private collections, were divided into many different greenhouses, each with a different regime of light, heat, and moisture for different seasons. Thus we had the Mexican House for cool mountain orchids from Central America, with their liking for a dry winter rest, and the Peruvian House, again cool but this time shady and very moist for orchids from the cloud forests of the Andes. In similar vein there was the hot East India House, the intermediate or Brazilian House, and so on.

By the end of the century orchids had ceased to be just for the very rich. Benjamin Williams and others had more or less developed the notions of modern orchid growing, and had divided orchids into three basic climatic types, to be grown in three greenhouses, or three divisions of a single house. These divisions are still used today, and with a little understanding of the natural habitat of our orchids, we can usually find a spot where most types will thrive.

Orchids fall into one of three divisions according to their temperature requirements and, particularly, to the minimum they will tolerate. Orchids for cool growing will tolerate a night winter minimum temperature of 50°F (10°C); intermediate orchids a temperature of 55°F (13°C); and warm growers a temperature of 65°F (18°C). But there are a few important reservations to be made. If the atmosphere and the plants are kept on the dry side, then no harm will result from temperatures 5°F (3°C) below these figures, so long as it is only for a short period. The drier they are the more cold they will survive, so dull, damp cold English winters are a problem, particularly if temperatures remain near the minimum for an extended period. Orchids are very tolerant and are hard to kill, but at the same time they are a challenge to grow really well. The gulf between surviving and thriving is wide. Orchids grown at the minimum temperature through weeks of dull winter weather will certainly not reward the grower with the best flowers.

There must be a temperature difference between day and night of approximately 10°F (5°C), and the same difference between summer and winter for both day and night temperatures. The sun may take care of these differences, but in dull weather the difference must be produced artificially. In summer the cool orchid house should, if possible, be prevented from rising much above 70°F (21°C) by shading, frequent damping down, and ventilation. It can be quite a challenge to keep a greenhouse at a lower temperature than outside, but efforts in this direction will certainly be rewarded. Although there is little chance of permanent damage to the plants below 90°F (32°C), the intermediate and warm houses should be kept below 80°F (26°C) as the metabolic rate of plants slows markedly above this temperature. The adverse effects of high temperatures are dehydration for plants that have a restricted root system, and can be minimized by maintaining as high a humidity as possible. Orchids like even conditions, and we must avoid hot and dry together, and cold and wet together.

Within a greenhouse there will always be areas that are a little cooler, or warmer, or shadier. Up near the ridge will be warmer, drier, and brighter, so by locating these areas, and understanding the orchids, growers can, with care and experience, grow some intermediate orchids in the cool house. Some cool-house orchids will do equally well grown in an intermediate house, but some will not.

Watering

Most orchids are epiphytes, and rain is soft and slightly acidic. Terrestrial orchids usually grow in humus-rich soils or leaf litter, which again tends to be acidic. There are some exceptions, notably some of the popular paphiopedilums, which grow on limestone cliffs, but most orchids grow in acidic conditions, so hard, alkaline tap water should be avoided. Chlorine in tap water is also to be avoided, so if tap water must be used it should be allowed to stand for a few hours, possibly overnight, before use. This will allow any chlorine to disperse, and also give the water time to reach greenhouse temperature.

By far the safest option is to use rainwater, and again to allow it to reach the temperature of the plants. If this option is not available then seek local advice, preferably from an experienced orchid grower. It may well be that the local tap water is perfectly satisfactory, but it is as well to check.

Orchid composts are such that it should not be possible for them to become waterlogged. Most of our orchids are epiphytes, and for them the most important ingredient in a compost is the air. If they do not like the compost they will rely on roots sent out into the air and, if that is not buoyantly humid, they will struggle. Get both the compost moisture and the air moisture right and the result is happy orchids.

Assuming the compost is suitable, then how often should orchids be watered? This is perhaps the most frequently asked question, particularly by beginners. The answer most often given, and the best answer, is 'as often as necessary', which, although accurate, is of little use. Orchids should be evenly moist when they are growing, usually in spring, summer, and autumn depending on variety, and drier if they are resting, usually in winter. As a general rule, orchids should be given a good soaking when they have nearly dried out from the last time. If in doubt carry on watering in spring and summer, wait until tomorrow if it is autumn, and leave it a few days longer in winter. In summer there will be little harm if orchids are soaking wet. In winter they should be drier, and those that have a total rest period can be allowed to dry out completely. Many orchids have this resting period, which may be a few weeks or may be many months, and many produce their flowers at the end of this rest. To flower at their best they require a cool, light, and dry position, and for convenience this rest period usually coincides with our winter. These orchids then flower in the late winter or spring.

Feeding

As a result of a rather nutrient-deficient lifestyle as epiphytes, most of our popular orchids are slow growing. They do not require a great deal of fertilizer, but as most orchid-compost mixes are devoid of nutrients, they must receive some fertilizer. Some growers mix a little slow-release general fertilizer with the compost, but the most popular method of feeding orchids is to use liquid fertilizer with the watering. General-purpose liquid plant feeds are quite satisfactory; they should be mixed half strength and used in spring and summer. In autumn many orchids benefit from a higher potash feed to help ripen the growths and to produce the best flowers. Special high-potash fertilizers are readily available, often labelled as tomato fertilizer.

Foliar feeding is often beneficial, especially immediately after repotting in the spring, when the plant may have few roots. It is as well to keep the compost on the dry side until a new root system is established, so foliar feeding can help to keep the plant going.

Potting

Repotting is necessary every two or three years, usually because the compost has decomposed and needs replacing rather than because the plant needs a larger pot. Orchids generally grow at their best when they appear to be in too small a pot, and the temptation to use a larger pot must be resisted. A large plant with many flower spikes is a wonderful sight, and although this is the aim of many amateurs, it is not produced by overpotting.

Potting time is usually at the end of the resting period, often immediately after flowering, when the new growth has started. Most orchids produce these new growths before they produce new roots, so to avoid damage to the new roots repotting is carried out just as they start to emerge from the new growth. If more plants are required then the plant can be carefully divided at this time. The rhizome must be located and cut to produce three bulb pieces, which can be potted separately into as small a size pot as appears comfortable.

Although many orchids, particularly warm-growing monopodials, do not have a resting period, they do slow down during winter when light becomes the limiting factor. They can be repotted at any time, but spring is perhaps still the best time.

All new acquisitions should be repotted into your favourite compost as soon as is convenient, as it is difficult to judge the watering of plants which are in different mixes.

Many plants can be grown on rafts of cork bark, or in wooden baskets. Indeed, some orchids seem to thrive when grown in this way, and for those that produce pendent flower spikes it is essential. A few plants grown this way add to the attraction of a mixed collection, and they have the advantage of taking no valuable space on what will certainly soon be crowded staging. They will need more frequent watering as they will dry out more rapidly than those in pots, and frequent spraying during the growing season will be beneficial.

There are almost as many different opinions about orchid composts as there are orchid growers, and many orchid growers change composts every time someone suggests something new.

As most orchids are epiphytes, the most important ingredient is air, so the compost must be open and well drained. It need not have any nutritional value but it must be neutral or slightly acid. Organic composts will eventually rot and become sour, particularly when nitrogen fertilizers are used, so long life is another important factor. Most modern composts are based either on coarse peat or pulverized pine bark, usually with the addition of coarse perlite. Some growers add charcoal, chopped sphagnum moss, or a variety of other ingredients. Whatever compost is used it should vary in coarseness according to the size of the plant and the diameter of its roots, with the coarsest used for plants with thick roots.

Propagation

Orchids are most easily propagated by simple division at repotting time and, as a general rule, divisions of sympodial orchids should be of three growths minimum. Orchids are slow-growing plants so it will not be possible to divide plants very often, and certainly not every year. Unless a division is required for a particular purpose my advice to amateurs is to try to grow large plants, as they are so much more impressive than a number of smaller individuals.

Monopodials such as vandas can become too tall, and can be propagated by cutting the top off, with some aerial roots attached, and potting up separately. Monopodials also produce side shoots, which can be separated from the main plant as soon as they have their own roots.

Some orchids produce what are known as keikis, the Hawaiian word for babies, which are small plants growing either on the old flower spikes (of phalaenopsis particularly), or on the canes of dendrobiums. Again these can be detached as soon as they have grown a few roots, and potted up separately. Some dendrobiums can also be propagated from sections of mature canes by laying them in a tray of compost in a warm and shady spot in the greenhouse.

All these are examples of vegetative propagation, that is the production of offspring identical to the parent plant, and they are all relatively slow. Over a number of years it may be possible to produce half a dozen plants from one. A new and desirable fuchsia or geranium can produce many thousands of cuttings in a short period, but new orchids always remained scarce and therefore expensive because propagation was so slow. However, the process of micropropagation has revolutionized the orchid industry, and now many thousands of identical plants can be produced from one. It still takes several years for the young plants to reach maturity, as it does from seed, but at least the numbers are theoretically unlimited. Most hybrid orchids are produced this way, but a few popular genera, notably paphiopedilums, remain reluctant to co-operate.

Sooner or later all orchid enthusiasts succumb to the temptation to have a go at breeding a new hybrid and raising the seedlings themselves, and certainly there is no thrill to compare with the anticipation as the first buds grow and open. The process will have taken several years, and will have needed a great deal of skill and care. The greenhouse will have produced less flowers than it could, as the growing seedlings demanded more and more space for themselves, and the results will probably be disappointing, but the fun is the anticipation, and the chance that something wonderful might result. Amateurs have produced really startling results from their breeding programmes, but the odds are stacked against it. However, if the urge to try is strong, then have a go.

First select the parents and check with the hybrid lists that the proposed hybrid has not already been made. Preferably choose a line of breeding that has not been explored, and which perhaps sounds a little unlikely. Commercial orchid breeders must to some extent play safe and avoid unlikely combinations, so there is scope for the amateur to have a go at more speculative crosses. To embark on similar lines to the professionals will almost certainly result in disappointment as they will have the best breeding stock and will in any case raise many thousands of seedlings to find the best. Choose an area where at least what is produced will be different, even if it is not very good!

The easy part is to place the pollen from one flower on the stigma of another. If there is a great difference in size between the two, then the pollen of the larger flower is more likely to fertilize the smaller flower than the other way round. If all goes well, a seed pod will form, swell and grow over several months, turning yellow and splitting when ripe. Not all seed pods contain seed, and it is not always easy to be sure as the seed is very fine. Commercially the seed is sown in sterile conditions on a nutrient-enriched agar jelly in glass flasks, and is grown for some time in these carefully controlled conditions. However, before such techniques were developed the method used was to sow the seed around the base of the mother plant. This is still a perfectly satisfactory method for an amateur who does not have the complex facilities for sterile asymbiotic culture, and who in any case requires only a few seedlings. Providing that care is taken with watering the seed may germinate and with luck a few seedlings will appear after several months. These can be potted up when large enough to handle and should flower several years later.

Pests and Diseases

Orchids are not particularly prone to pests and diseases, and are certainly less trouble than many other greenhouse plants. Strong healthy plants produced by good cultivation methods will attract fewer problems than those that are sickly and struggling. Scrupulous cleanliness in the green-house also helps and an annual autumn clean out offers the opportunity for a close inspection of each plant. General good housekeeping prevents many problems from arising.

Slugs and snails, scale insects, aphids, and mealy bugs are reasonably easily controlled by proprietary chemicals, always used exactly as suggested by the manufacturers. More difficult is red spider, which is in fact neither red nor a spider, but which can be a problem, particularly on cymbidiums. Red spiders are very small yellowish mites that damage leaves, particularly on the undersides, and can breed at an alarming rate before they are noticed. There are several sprays available, but some seem to be ineffec-tive in some areas, and the best advice will be obtained from an experienced local orchid grower. Conditions certainly play a part, and a dry atmosph-ere seems to suit red spider more than a humid one. As orchids prefer high humidity, red spider should not get out of hand, and when it does it usually indicates that the atmosphere is too dry.

There are a number of fungal infections and rots that can affect orchids, but fortunately they are rarely fatal. A spray with a proprietary fungicide will usually suffice, but should not be used too often as orchids sometimes react by slowing their growth rate. Bacterial rots are rather more serious and are more easily prevented with clean and tidy conditions and good culture than cured afterwards. As with fungal infections the damaged parts of the plant should be cut away with a sterilized knife and the cuts treated with sulphur.

Sooner or later the convert to orchid growing will encounter the dreaded word 'virus'. Orchids suffer their share of virus diseases and, as in most plants, the disease is unsightly to us and debilitating for the plant. Although a plant weakened by virus disease is certainly more susceptible to pests and other pro-blems, virus diseases are rarely fatal, and this presents a problem. We see so much virus about because so many growers do not recognize the disease, and the plants do not die. The symptoms to look out for are pale streaks in the leaves, maybe turning brown or black with secondary fungal infections, and streaking and blotching of colour in the flowers. Always seek expert advice if there is any doubt, and never purchase a plant nor accept as a gift a plant if there are any doubtful markings. If it is confirmed or even reasonably suspected by an expert, then burn any plant with virus. This may seem harsh advice but there is no cure and the disease does spread.

Virus diseases are spread by infection of the sap of one plant by the sap of an infected plant. Aphids and other sap-sucking insects have been blamed, but perhaps more disease is spread by orchid growers themselves. Always sterilize knives between jobs when cutting flowers and dividing plants. With all the pests and diseases the best approach is preven-tion. Good, healthy, and vigorous plants grown in well-regulated and clean conditions by an enthusiast who understands their requirements are unlikely to succumb.

SPECIES ORCHIDS

Ada

The genus *Ada* was until quite recently considered to be monotypic, that is with only one species, but a few members of the genus *Brassia* have been re-classified and are now included in this genus. However, it is the original member, *Ada aurantiaca*, that is by far the best known, and certainly deserves a place in a mixed cool-house collection.

These species come from the cool mountain forests of Central and South America, where they grow as epiphytes. They are easily grown and thrive in much the same conditions as odontoglossums. *Ada aurantiaca* produces its attractive orange flowers in winter and spring, and soon grows into a specimen plant with many spikes if the temptation to divide the plant is resisted. The nodding bell-shaped flowers do not open fully, and are quite unlike most orchids. At one time this most unusual orchid was quite scarce in cultivation but in recent years it has been raised from seed, and so is now readily available. Not only is this a good thing from the conservation viewpoint, but also because captive raised plants seem to grow so much more easily, and the flowers are often superior to wild collected plants, as they are raised from the best available parents.

In spite of the fact that adas are closely related to odontoglossums, only a few hybrids have been produced to date.

Aërangis

There are more than fifty members of this genus found growing as woodland epiphytes throughout tropical Africa and Madagascar. They are small monopodial plants mostly with white or pale-coloured flowers borne on long racemes, and with one exception are rarely seen in cultivation.

The exception is the delightful *Aërangis rhodosticta*, which comes from the lower montane forests of Central and East Africa. It is most easily grown on a raft of cork bark, where its pendent spikes of white flowers with their characteristic red eye are displayed at their best. A warm and humid spot in the intermediate house, or better still with *Phalaenopsis* in the warm house, suits this orchid. This most desirable species was formerly quite rare in cultivation, and therefore rather expensive, but thankfully it is now being raised from seed.

Aërides

These attractive monopodial orchids produce pendent spikes of showy white or pink flowers, and are sometimes known as foxtail orchids. There are several species in the genus, all from southeast Asia, and all require warm, moist, and shady conditions during the summer. In winter they need as much light as possible, and will tolerate intermediate temperatures if kept on the dry side. They produce numerous thick but rather fragile aerial roots, and are best left undisturbed in a wooden basket, where the roots can hang freely in the air. Most species produce long-lasting and sweetly scented flowers in late spring and summer.

The beautiful pink-flowered *Aërides fieldingii*, and *A. odoratum*, which is usually white, are the species most likely to be seen in cultivation, and both can be recommended.

Angraecum

There are upwards of two hundred species of *Angraecum* distributed throughout tropical central and southern Africa, with several in Madagascar and the adjacent islands. They are monopodial epiphytes and require warm, and humid conditions.

All have white or white and green flowers, some delightfully scented, with nectar spurs of varying length produced as backward extensions of the base of the lip. The most common in cultivation are the large species from Madagascar.

Angraecum sesquipedale, sometimes known as the star of Bethlehem, is perhaps the best-known member of the genus. The large, ivory-white, star-shaped flowers are delicately scented and are produced around Christmas. Each flower has a hollow spur up to 1ft 6in (45cm) long, and the nectar at the end can only be reached by an insect with a proboscis of this length. The smaller-flowered *A. eburneum* is also deservedly popular with amateurs, producing spikes of inverted green and white blooms in winter.

There are some hybrid angraecums, the best known of which is *A.* Veitchii, a cross between *A. sesquipedale* and *A. eburneum*, first made in 1899 by Veitch. It combines qualities from both its parents and is often thought to be easier to grow than either, eventually producing a large plant.

Anguloa

The genus *Anguloa* consists of ten or so epiphytic or terrestrial species from the mountains of South America. They are all quite large deciduous plants, related and similar in structure to lycastes. However, the flowers are quite different, being cup- or tulip-shaped – they are often known as tulip orchids. They are sometimes called cradle orchids, because the lip is so loosely hinged that it rocks gently whenever the flower is disturbed.

These orchids are easily grown in a rich, fibrous compost in cool conditions, where they bloom in early spring. Flowers are borne singly on upright stems rising, often several together, from the base of the bare pseudobulbs. Being deciduous they should have a dry, cool rest in winter, and need not be watered until the new growths are well advanced in the spring. The large deciduous leaves are quite thin and easily scorched, so they must be shaded.

Anguloa uniflora, with pink spotted flowers, and *A. ruckeri*, with green flowers spotted red inside, are quite popular, but the favourite is *A. clowesii*. This produces large, fragrant, yellow tulip-shaped flowers during the spring, and nursery-raised plants are now readily available.

Hybrids have been made, particularly intergeneric hybrids with lycastes. These are vigorous and easily grown orchids combining the size and substance of the *Anguloa* flowers with the open shape of the *Lycaste*. There are many of these hybrids about, and they are almost all attractive and scented, but perhaps the best known is the yellow *Angulocaste* Olympus.

Anoectochilus

There are more than thirty species in this genus, which is found throughout southeast Asia, from the Himalayas to the islands of the Pacific. Terrestrial creepers, they inhabit forest floors.

These beautiful orchids are usually grown for their foliage rather than their flowers, and make an interesting addition to a warm-house collection. They are, however, not easy plants to grow well. They should be grown in a rich but perfectly drained compost in shallow pans in a humid and shady part of a warm greenhouse. They dislike draughts, and are often most successful under a bell jar, or in an indoor growing case.

Few species are available in cultivation, but those most likely to be seen are *Anoectochilus roxburghii* and the similar *A. sikkimensis*, both from northern India.

Ansellia

The two species of *Ansellia* may be in fact the same species, but, whether or not this is so, they are likely to be met under the names *Ansellia africana* or *A. gigantea*.

These robust epiphytic plants grow much like evergreen dendrobiums, with clumps of cane-like pseudobulbs. They are widespread in tropical Africa, and are quite variable, with flowers ranging from small, pale yellow to large, deep yellow, heavily spotted with rich brown – markings that have given them their common name of leopard orchid. To be sure of obtaining a good form these orchids should be purchased in flower, or as divisions of a known variety.

Ansellias need warm conditions with a dry rest in winter and lots of light to ripen the pseudobulbs. The branched flower spikes are produced, often in large numbers, in spring and summer and a good form in full bloom can be a glorious sight.

Arachnis

This genus consists of about six species of monopodial climbing epiphytes found throughout southeast Asia. The only species likely to be seen in cultivation is *Arachnis flos-aëris*, sometimes known as the scorpion orchid.

The plant can reach several feet in length and, as it needs plenty of light in warm greenhouse conditions, it is not easy to accommodate. The striking yellow and maroon flowers are produced on branched spikes, and last well on the plant or cut. Many hybrids with other related vandaceous genera have been made, particularly in the Far East, where they are produced and grown in large quantities to supply cut flowers for the international trade.

Arundina

Often known as the bamboo orchid, several species have been described, but it may well be that they are all forms of a single highly variable species. *Arundina graminifolia* is found from India and China through southeast Asia to the Pacific islands. It grows in large clumps, very much like bamboo, up to 8ft (2.5m) tall, with terminal mauve flowers produced in succession in summer.

It should be grown in a large pot, or directly into a bed, in a warm greenhouse. It is an interesting novelty, but only for those who have plenty of room.

Barkeria

There are about ten species of *Barkeria*, found growing as epiphytes in the forests of Central America. Some authorities classify them in the genus *Epidendrum*, with which they are at least closely related.

The two species most likely to be seen in cultivation are the purple-flowered *Barkeria skinneri* and the paler *B. spectabilis*. These compact species require intermediate conditions with plenty of moisture and light during the summer. In autumn they shed some of their leaves and need a cool, dry rest during which they flower. They can be grown in pots or baskets but often thrive when mounted on a slab of tree fern or cork bark.

Bifrenaria

There are perhaps twenty or so species of *Bifrenaria* from Central and northern South America where they grow as epiphytes or terrestrials. They are closely related to lycastes, and should be grown in cool or intermediate conditions in much the same way as this genus. Unlike lycastes they retain their tough leathery leaves through the winter, but like their relatives they must have a cool and very dry rest, even to the point of shrivelling the pseudobulbs.

The most familiar species is *Bifrenaria harrisoniae*, a species from Brazil. It is among the easiest of orchids to grow well, and produces its heavily textured, cream flowers in spring. The flowers have a purple lip covered with hairs, and a strong perfume.

Other members of the genus that may be seen are the yellow-flushed, red-flowered *B. atropurpurea*, and the purple-flowered *B. tyrianthina*. These are also from Brazil and both deserve a place in a mixed cool collection.

Bletilla

Although there are several species of *Bletilla* found in eastern Asia, only one is familiar in cultivation. *Bletilla striata* from China, Japan, and Tibet is perfectly hardy outdoors if protected from the effects of very hard frosts and extreme wet. It is, however, at its best in a pot in a cold alpine house, where its delicate purple flowers are not damaged by spring rain.

The deciduous pseudobulbs should be planted 1–2in (2.5–5cm) deep and left undisturbed. They are readily available from normal horticultural outlets, but are often erroneously labelled as *Bletia*, a tropical genus which comes from Central and South America and which they superficially resemble.

Brassavola

There are fifteen or so members of this genus, found throughout tropical Central and South America from Mexico to Argentina. They are mainly epiphytic and are grown in intermediate conditions very much like cattleyas, but with a dry and light winter rest. Several popular species are pendent and are best grown in a basket, or on a piece of tree fern or cork bark. Most have green, yellow, or white flowers, often strongly scented and particularly so in the evening, and usually produced in summer.

Brassavola nodosa and *B. cucullata* are just two species which are worthy of a place in an orchid collection, but there are several others also.

B. digbyana and *B. glauca* are more robust and upright, rather like laelias, and are sometimes classified in the genus *Rhyncholaelia*. *B. digbyana* has the most spectacular, large, scented flowers of the genus. It is often grown on a raft, but is never easy, and can be particularly reluctant to flower. Its many intergeneric hybrids are usually more colourful and certainly more reliable. The large lip has a deep fringe, which is inherited by its hybrids. Almost all the *Brassocattleyas*, *Brassolaeliocattleyas*, and other related intergeneric hybrids involve this species.

Brassia

These orchids, often known as spider orchids, are very popular with amateur growers, and always create a stir when seen in public. There are twenty or so species from Central and South America and although they all have the characteristic spidery flowers it is the species with very long sepals that are most often seen in collections. They are easily grown in intermediate conditions, rather like oncidiums or the warmer growing odontoglossums to which they are related.

Brassia verrucosa from Mexico has large, greenish-yellow flowers and will tolerate cooler conditions. *B. gireoudeana* is also popular, but the most spectacular member of the genus is *B. longissima* with yellow and brown flowers often over 1ft (30cm) long from tip of sepal to tip of sepal.

In recent years there has been increasing interest in breeding brassias with their cousins the odontoglossums, oncidiums, and miltonias. The results have been mixed, but among the best have been the maclellanaras, notably *Maclellanara* Pagan Lovesong, several clones of which have won awards around the world. Some of these clones changed hands until quite recently for large sums of money, but thanks to micropropagation the best of these are now available at reasonable prices.

Bulbophyllum

Several authorities maintain this to be the largest of all orchid genera, with some two thousand species. Some split it up into other genera, leaving about a thousand true bulbophyllums. In either case it is a very variable genus of mainly tropical epiphytes, found throughout tropical America, Africa, and Australasia, with the largest number in southeast Asia.

Bulbophyllums are mostly small plants, and all have fascinating flowers. They are certainly not beautiful in the normal sense, and many have absolutely revolting perfumes, but they are intriguing. Examination with a hand lens often reveals flowers with mobile lips or parts of the lip, or very mobile hairs, all presumably related to the pollination mechanism.

It is difficult to recommend the best from so many but *Bulbophyllum barbigerum* is a good example of flowers with mobile and hairy parts to the lip. Others sometimes seen are *B. collettii* and *B. lobbii*.

Calanthe

The hundred and fifty or so species of *Calanthe* are tropical terrestrial plants found mainly in Asia, with a few species in Africa and South America. The genus is divided into deciduous species and evergreen species, and both types require warm, moist, and shady conditions, with the deciduous types needing a dry and cooler rest when they are leafless.

Calanthe vestita is perhaps the best known, and is deciduous. The flowers range from white to deep pink and are produced on long, arching spikes from the bare pseudobulbs during the winter. When the new growth starts after flowering the pseudobulbs should be potted in a rich compost, and fed throughout the growing season.

There are many evergreen types, all of which are attractive. Among the best are *C. masuca*, with deep mauve flowers, and *C. rosea*, with delicate pink blooms.

Catasetum

Catasetums are very curious orchids. There are about fifty species from tropical Central and South America and most have the strange habit of producing separate male and female flowers, often on separate spikes and at different times. These flowers are so dissimilar that early botanists thought that they were dealing with different species, and often classified them in different genera.

Most species need intermediate conditions, and with their pendulous flower spikes they do well in baskets. Many eject their pollen masses with considerable force when the trigger antennae are touched.

Catasetum pileatum has large, white or yellow, fragrant flowers and is the national flower of Venezuela. Quite recently a new form with deep wine-red flowers has been discovered. Other species sometimes seen are *C. fimbriatum*, which has green flowers spotted with brown and a fringed lip, and *C. maculatum*.

Chysis

These robust epiphytic orchids are found from Mexico to Peru, and, of the six species in the genus, four are rarely seen in cultivation. The two familiar species are pendulous in habit and are best grown in a basket, or on a raft, in cool or intermediate conditions. They are semi-deciduous and benefit from a dry winter rest.

Chysis aurea produces spikes of up to eight fragrant yellow flowers from the base of the maturing growth. *C. bractescens* flowers in a similar way but has somewhat larger, fragrant, white flowers.

Cirrhopetalum

There are upwards of thirty species of cirrhopetalums distributed through southeast Asia from India to the Pacific islands, with a few in Africa. They are often included in the genus *Bulbophyllum*, and most make interesting additions to an intermediate house collection. As they produce scrambling plants they are best accommodated in a basket.

Cirrhopetalum medusae from Malaya has small flowers with very extended sepals, which give the inflorescence the appearance of a hairy pom-pom. Also with extended sepals are two similar species, *C. rothschildianum* and *C. longissimum*. Although these are rarely seen, a fine clone of the vigorous hybrid between them has recently been micropropagated. This splendid orchid, *C.* Elizabeth Ann 'Bucklebury', is a must for anyone fascinated by the unusual.

Cochlioda

There are six species of these small orchids from the high Andes of Ecuador, Peru, and Bolivia, which have been used extensively to bring their bright red colouring to hybrid odontoglossums.

They are small plants with small bright flowers. The best known by far is the vibrant red *Cochlioda noezliana*, but the pink *C. rosea* is sometimes seen. Coming from high altitude they require cool and bright conditions, and possibly because it is difficult to provide light without heat, they have the reputation of being difficult to grow well, and very difficult to flower. However, clones do appear to vary considerably and some growers do very well with these orchids.

More reliable by far for the amateur are the early primary hybrids, which retain the delicate character of the species. It is a testament to their toughness, in direct contrast to their parent, that they still survive, probably from the original matings around the turn of the century. Examples to look out for are *Odontioda* Cooksoniae, Keighleyensis, Charlesworthii, and Bradshawiae, or, a further generation on from *Odontioda* Charlesworthii, the wonderful old red hybrid *Vuylstekeara* Edna.

Coelogyne

Very few of the hundred and more species of *Coelogyne* fail to be worthy of a place in an orchid collection. They are found throughout southeast Asia, where they grow as epiphytes. Most have white flowers, often with yellow markings on the lip.

For horticultural purposes we can divide the genus into those from high altitudes in India and Burma, which we grow in the cool house, and the generally larger species from the tropical areas, which we grow in the warm house. There are a few that require intermediate conditions.

One of the all-time favourite orchids of amateurs over the years is *Coelogyne cristata*. This beautiful white and yellow orchid is often grown successfully as a house plant, spending its winter rest in an unheated part of the house, but is equally at home in a cool greenhouse. Other cool-growing favourites include the richly scented *C. ochracea* and the pendulous, cream-flowered *C. massangeana*.

Perhaps the most sought-after species is *C. pandurata*, the black orchid. It must be grown in warm, shady, and moist conditions and produces green flowers with black markings on the lip. More often seen, and easier to grow, is the very similar hybrid between this species and *C. asperata*, called *C.* Burfordiensis.

Among the intermediate coelogynes, the species *C. mooreana*, particularly the variety 'Brockhurst', can be recommended, as can *C.* Mem. W. Micholitz, a hybrid from it.

Colax

The only species likely to be seen in cultivation is *Colax jugosus*, now botanically known as *Pabstia jugosa*, but still more commonly known by its old name. It comes from Brazil and is fairly easy to grow in intermediate conditions, producing its purple-blotched white flowers in spring.

Although quite an attractive orchid in its own right, its main claim to fame is as one of the few blue orchids, although it is fair to say that some imagination is needed to see blue in what is at best a violet purple. It has been hybridized successfully with zygopetalums, another near-blue genus, and some interesting *Zygocolax* hybrids have been produced.

Comparettia

These colourful little relatives of the oncidiums are not as often seen as they deserve. The genus contains about twelve species, from Central and South America, and they are often reported as being rather temperamental plants to grow. They need shady conditions in the intermediate house, and seem to do best on a raft of tree fern or cork bark. They have small pseudobulbs so should never be allowed to dry out completely.

Comparettia macroplectron, with its delicate pink flowers, is perhaps the best known, but also worthy of mention are the brilliant orange-flowered *C. speciosa* and *C. coccinea*.

In recent years a number of brightly coloured hybrids have been produced, particularly with rodriguezias and odontoglossums, and these may be more accommodating than the species.

Cycnoches

About twelve species of this fascinating genus are found growing as epiphytes or occasionally as terrestrials in the American tropics. Although normal flowers are produced, they generally produce male and female flowers on separate spikes at different times, or sometimes on the same spike. In some species these male and female flowers are quite similar, whereas with other species they may be quite different.

They should be grown in a warm greenhouse, and need a cooler, dry rest immediately after flowering, usually in autumn. Care should be taken with watering, particularly immediately after this rest period, as the pseudobulbs are prone to rotting.

The most common species, and perhaps the best, is *Cycnoches chlorochilon*, with large yellowish green flowers, the curved column of which gives these orchids their common name of swan orchids. With this species the male and female flowers are quite similar, whereas *C. egertonianum* is a good example of the type with different flowers.

Cymbidiella

There are three members of this genus, all rather cymbidium-like in their growth, and all native to the island of Madagascar. They are subjects for the warm house, where they need moderate shade and moisture and absolutely perfect drainage. They have always had the reputation for being difficult in cultivation, but with the correct treatment they can be vigorous, producing their startling flowers in summer.

All cymbidiellas are rare, and probably threatened with extinction in the wild, but the best-known species, *Cymbidiella rhodochila*, has been successfully raised from seed several times, so young plants are available. Its flowers are vivid green, with black green spots on the petals and a most striking crimson lip.

Cypripedium

Formerly all the slipper orchids were included in this genus, but with the removal of the tropical species to the genus *Paphiopedilum*, the true cypripediums now number about twenty-five species. They are found growing as terrestrials, often in shady and moist woodlands, in north temperate Asia, Japan, Europe, and North America.

They are mostly hardy plants, providing that they are protected from the worst frosts. Soil requirements vary from species to species, and some are easier to grow than others. *Cypripedium acaule* and *C. reginae*, both from North America, are relatively easy. Do not be tempted by dry roots of *C. calceolus*, which are sometimes offered for sale. They rarely survive and in any case may well have been illegally dug up from the wild.

Dendrobium

This is one of the largest genera of orchids, with about nine hundred species, among them very many attractive and popular plants. They are found from India, China, and Japan through all southeast Asia to Australia and the Pacific islands including New Zealand. They are mostly epiphytes and range from less than 2in (5cm) high to over 15ft (4.5m). Some are evergreen and some deciduous, and many produce plantlets from the nodes of the cane-like pseudobulbs, which can be removed and potted up as soon as they have developed a good root system.

For horticultural purposes we can divide the genus into several sections, each requiring different treatment.

The first section is a large group of high-altitude species from India and Burma. These grow well in a cool house and flower in the spring if given a cool, dry, and light winter rest and a warm, humid growing season. The pendulous pink-flowered species *Dendrobium pierardii*, also known botanically as *D. aphyllum*, is a favourite with

growers, but *D. nobile*, with white and mauve flowers, is perhaps the best known of this group. Many spectacular hybrids in a variety of colours have been produced, particularly in Hawaii, from these species. They are found under the name of their breeder as Yamamoto Dendrobiums, and these orchids are becoming popular with amateurs.

Also cool growing is a group of white-flowered dendrobiums with canes covered in characteristic black hairs. This group includes the popular *D. infundibulum* and *D. williamsonii*. Another favourite for this type of culture is the all-yellow *D. densiflorum* and its close relative *D. thyrsiflorum* with white petals and sepals. These two have canes with a square cross section and produce large, multi-flowered, pendulous spikes in spring.

Another group, of warm-growing hybrids, owes its origin to a number of tropical species, notably the Australian Cookstown Orchid, *D. phalaenopsis*, together with the similar *D. bigibbum*. These hybrids are seen in a variety of shades of mauve and purple, and are bred and grown extensively as cut flowers alongside vandas for export, particularly in Thailand.

Also warm growing are the New Guinea hybrids, mostly bred from *D. stratiotes*, *D. antennatum* and *D. taurinum*, the bull orchid. These flowers, with their elongated and twisted petals, are often known collectively as antelope orchids, and they are also grown for the cut-flower trade.

A further group comes from the temperate mountains of eastern Australia. These species are easy to grow in cool, light conditions and soon form large plants. *D. kingianum*, with many small mauve flowers produced in spring after a dry winter rest, is a favourite. In recent years a number of interesting hybrids have been produced in Australia from various species in this group.

Dendrochilum

There are over a hundred and twenty species of *Dendrochilum* found throughout tropical southeast Asia. The greatest concentration is in the mountains of Sumatra and Borneo, but many of these species are rarely seen in cultivation. The three more common members of the genus all come from the Philippines, and are quite similar in structure.

Although these orchids originate in a warm climate, they thrive in an intermediate greenhouse, and often do well in a cool collection so long as they are kept dry during the winter. They produce clustered pseudobulbs, each with a single leaf, and are at their best when allowed to form a large plant in a shallow pot or basket. The cream or yellowish flowers are small, but are produced in large numbers on long arching spikes, which give them the popular name of chain orchid. Perhaps the most striking feature of these orchids is their attractive and very strong perfume.

The three species that can be recommended are *Dendrochilum cobbianum*, which flowers in autumn, and *D. filiforme* and *D. glumaceum*, which flower in spring.

Disa

There are about a hundred and thirty species of *Disa* distributed throughout tropical Africa, with a concentration of species in South Africa. They are all terrestrials with tuberous roots and, although many have attractive flowers, they are, with one exception, little known outside their homeland.

The exception is the spectacular *Disa uniflora*, often known as the pride of Table Mountain, which has large, bright red flowers. This orchid was popular toward the end of the last century, when it was often successfully grown in general plant collections. Indeed, the advice at the time was to treat it as if it were a geranium!

After World War I it appears to have become rare in cultivation, and until quite recently it was regarded as almost impossible to grow. This may have been because its culture is quite unlike most exotic orchids, and if treated as a cool-house species it certainly does struggle. In recent years it has been raised from seed, and plants are now generally available.

D. uniflora grows up to 4,000ft (1,200m) above sea level, at which altitude it may be subject to frost. It is usually found at the sides of streams, and particularly around waterfalls, where it is constantly wet at the roots, and the atmosphere is locally humid. The flowers are produced in early summer, when they are subjected to direct bright sunlight, but the leaves are usually in the shade of streamside vegetation and the roots remain moist and cool. In cultivation disas require an open, acid compost and moist, frost-free conditions.

Several hybrids were made around the turn of the century, using this species with other, closely related and more floriferous species such as *D. tripetaloides*. Recently there has been renewed interest in this large genus, and many of the old hybrids have been remade. Indeed, many new hybrids have also been produced, and although *D. uniflora* remains tricky, the hybrids can be recommended.

Doritis

There are only two or three members of this genus of monopodial orchids, and they are found in the warm forests of southeast Asia, from India through Thailand to Sumatra. They are related to *Phalaenopsis*, and thrive in similar warm conditions, but they tend to grow a little taller.

The most common member of the genus is *Doritis pulcherrima*, which has hard, greyish leaves spotted with purple. The small flowers vary from dark purple through shades of pink, with a bluish form and a white albino being particularly sought after. The upright spikes produce a succession of flowers over a long period, and well-grown specimens can be in bloom all year.

The dark forms of *D. pulcherrima* have been used extensively in breeding with *Phalaenopsis* to produce deep pink hybrids.

Dracula

Until recently these orchids were included in the genus *Masdevallia*, and some authorities still include them there. However, for no other reason than the wonderfully descriptive name, I will consider them separately.

These fascinating and sometimes sinister-looking orchids inhabit the humid mountain forests of Central and South America and should be grown in shady and humid conditions in a cool house. As the flowers are often produced downward they are best grown in an open compost in baskets. Because they have no pseudobulbs, they need to be moist all year round.

Perhaps the best-known member of the genus is *Dracula chimaera*, which has large, three-tailed flowers covered in black hairs. It is worth growing for the reaction it produces when shown to non-orchid growers – most find its appearance quite evil! The similar *D. vampira* must be included, if only for its wonderfully descriptive name. Less frightening is the popular *D. bella*, with cream flowers covered in crimson spots.

Dryadella

These tiny orchids, often known as partridge-in-the-grass orchids have also been recently removed from the genus *Masdevallia*. There are several members of the genus, all quite similar, and mostly from Brazil. They should be grown in the same cool-house conditions as their close relatives.

Dryadella zebrina, with crimson-spotted green flowers, is perhaps the most common in collections, but the yellowish flowers of *D. edwallii* are sometimes seen. One of the smallest of all, and one of the gems of the genus, is *D. lilliputana*, with red-spotted cream flowers.

Encyclia

Although the genus *Encyclia* was established as long ago as 1828, most members have for many years been included in *Epidendrum*. The two genera were separated relatively recently, most of those with pseudobulbs being transferred to the genus *Encyclia*.

The hundred and fifty or so members of this genus are found mainly in Mexico, with some in the West Indies, Central America and South America. Most come from mountainous areas, and are relatively easy to grow in cool conditions, and several are attractively perfumed, some powerfully so. Of these *Encyclia fragrans*, with cream or greenish flowers, can be recommended.

E. cochleata is a deserved favourite with beginners, and is amongst the easiest of all orchids to grow, often as a house plant. The spikes of curious green and purple flowers continue to elongate for many months, and well-grown plants are seldom without some flowers. The bright scarlet flowers of *E. vitellina*, another favourite, are a welcome sight in spring in a cool-house collection.

Two other Mexican species deserve a special mention, although neither is quite as easy to grow as the others. *E. citrina*, still often referred to as *Cattleya citrina*, grows upside down, and is best cultivated on a piece of bark. In spring, after a long rest, it produces one or two large, waxy yellow flowers with the scent of lemons from each new growth. Its relative, *E. mariae*, has similar glaucous leaves, but grows upright. Again the flowers are large for such a small plant, and in this case are yellowish green with a huge white lip.

Epidendrum

This is one of the largest genera of orchids, with many hundreds of species, perhaps as many as a thousand, widely distributed throughout the tropical Americas from North Carolina to Argentina. Most are reed-stemmed plants, flowering terminally, but there are some with pseudobulbs.

The name is derived from the Greek *epi* (upon) and *dendron* (tree), which refers to the epiphytic habit of most species. Before about 1800 most epiphytic orchids were placed in this genus, regardless of their relationships, so the genus has undergone many revisions since. Those remaining continue to be reviewed and divided by taxonomists.

One of the best known of all tropical orchids is *Epidendrum ibaguense*, a reed-stemmed species found throughout tropical America. With such a wide distribution considerable variation might be expected, and indeed there are plants with flowers of red, magenta, orange, yellow, and white. The red form is often still known as *E. radicans*. It is so easy to grow in almost any conditions that I doubt whether there are many orchid collections anywhere without a plant, and most orchid growers are happy to part with a piece for a beginner.

A similar, but decidedly warm-growing species, is *E. pseudepidendrum* from Costa Rica and Panama. This species is becoming quite rare in the wild, but happily is easy to raise from seed. The flowers are quite firm and solid, as if made from hard plastic, and the colour combination of vivid green sepals and petals with a bright orange and magenta lip usually produces gasps of amazement when first seen.

Among the many other notable species are *E. ciliare*, often grown for its fringed and scented pale yellow flowers, *E. medusae* for its curious red and purple fringed flowers, and *E. stamfordianum* for its long spikes of spotted pale green and white flowers.

Epigeneium

There are about thirty-five species in this genus, distributed from India through southeast Asia. Most are curious rather than beautiful, often with quite large flowers, but few species are generally available.

Epigeneium amplum is perhaps the most popular, with large, solitary, brown flowers produced in the autumn from the apex of each new pseudobulb. It has rather a scruffy habit, with the pseudobulbs well spaced out along an ascending rhizome, which makes it difficult to accommodate in a pot. It is best grown in the cool house, on a piece of bark.

Eria

Although a large and variable genus of over five hundred species, distributed throughout tropical southeast Asia, erias are rarely seen in collections. Many are rather insignificant, but there are some that deserve wider cultivation, particularly as they are generally easy to grow if given shady and humid conditions in an intermediate or warm greenhouse.

Eria coronaria is a beautiful cool-growing species from India. The delicately scented, cream-coloured flowers are produced in spikes of three to five from the apex of the canes in spring. *E. javanica* has a more conventionally shaped pseudobulb, from the apex a long spike of many attractive white and yellow flowers is produced. It flowers in late winter, and prefers warm conditions.

Eulophia

A large and little-cultivated genus of over two hundred species of mainly terrestrial orchids from tropical central and southern Africa. The genus can be roughly divided into two groups. Those with pear-shaped pseudobulbs and deciduous foliage generally have flowers with a large lip, whereas more evenly shaped flowers are produced by the group with thin pseudobulbs and evergreen leaves.

A popular member of the first group is *Eulophia guineensis*. It produces attractive flowers with dull, purple, re-curving sepals and petals, and a large delicate pink lip. It should be grown in a warm greenhouse, but a cooler lighter and drier rest in winter is beneficial.

Members of the second group are rarely seen in cultivation, but *E. paiveana* can be recommended for its bright yellow flowers.

Galeandra

These attractive orchids are rarely seen in collections, but deserve to be better known. There are about twenty species, many quite similar, distributed throughout the American tropics. They are quite easy orchids to grow in intermediate conditions with a cooler and drier winter rest.

Galeandra baueri is one of the best, and is the type species of the genus. Plants are often named after their discoverers, or to honour some notable botanist or aristocrat. The botanical artists of the past, and indeed of the present, are usually forgotten, but this species is a rare exception. It was named in honour of Francis Bauer (1748–1840), whose work is for me the finest of all botanical art.

Gomesa

Brazil is the home of twenty or so species in this genus. They are pseudobulbous epiphytes that, with their pale green foliage, resemble rather anaemic odontoglossums.

With the possible exception of *Gomesa recurva*, the only species commonly seen in cultivation is the deservedly popular *G. crispa*. This species produces long arching spikes of small yellow-green flowers, often several from each pseudobulb. The main attraction of the flowers is the delightful perfume.

Gongora

These orchids are flatteringly called interesting or fascinating, but perhaps a more accurate description would be grotesque. The rather dully coloured yellow or buff flowers, often with spots, are produced on a pendulous spike from the base of the pseudobulbs. They must therefore be cultivated in baskets, in much the same way as their relatives in the genus *Stanhopea*.

There are about twenty-five species in this Central and South American genus, but only *Gongora quinquenervis* and *G. galeata* are commonly seen. Both species are highly scented, with the former producing a spicy and pungent perfume, and the latter a perfume said to resemble oranges. They are worth growing for their perfume and for their curiosity value.

Grammangis

There are only two species in this genus, both endemic to Madagascar. They are robust epiphytes, related to and similar in plant structure to *Cymbidiella*. They need warm greenhouse conditions and are said to resent disturbance.

Grammangis ellisii produces arching spikes of rich, brownish, scented flowers in summer. The sepals are large and the petals quite small, which gives them a triangular shape rather like a lycaste.

Huntleya

There may be up to ten different species in this interesting tropical American genus, but only one is at all common in cultivation.

Huntleya meleagris, which is also known as *H. burtii*, grows without pseudobulbs. The leaves are produced from an upright stem and form a fan, with single flowers from between the leaves. These are quite large and very waxy, with brownish-yellow sepals and petals, and a reddish-brown and white lip. Huntleyas have the reputation of being rather difficult in cultivation, and are prone to rotting in conditions that are too warm and humid. They should not be divided or disturbed unless absolutely necessary.

Ionopsis

The few species in this genus range throughout the tropical and subtropical Americas from Florida to Paraguay. The name of the genus is derived from the Greek *ion* (violet), because the flowers resemble those of violets. *Opsis*, which occurs in many names, means appearance. They are closely related to the genus *Comparettia*.

These small epiphytic orchids deserve to be grown more widely than they are. The species most likely to be seen is *Ionopsis utricularioides*, with attractive pale pink, lavender, or even magenta flowers.

Laelia

There are about fifty species in this genus, among them some of the most popular of all orchids. They are mostly epiphytes from Mexico south to Peru and Brazil. The genus is divided into several sections, three of which are of particular interest.

The first group is from Mexico, and its members thrive in cool conditions with plenty of light, particularly during the winter resting period. They are all easy to grow, producing attractive and long-lasting mauve flowers. *Laelia autumnalis* flowers in autumn and *L. anceps* in winter. Also flowering usually in winter is perhaps the finest of this group *L. gouldiana*. It may be that this is a natural hybrid between the other two, or it may be that it is just a more richly coloured form of *L. autumnalis*, or is indeed a separate species. Whatever its origins, it is a must for a cool greenhouse, and is often seen growing successfully as a house plant.

The second group consists of a number of taller-growing species, mainly from Brazil, with large cattleya-like flowers. Most often seen is the national flower of Brazil, *Laelia purpurata*, which flowers in spring, and should be grown with cattleyas in an intermediate greenhouse. There are many colour forms of this popular orchid, including rare and beautiful bluish varieties. As with all variable species there are some miserable varieties, so care must be taken when purchasing plants.

Finally there is a group of smaller-flowered species, again from Brazil, with bright yellow or orange flowers. They require intermediate greenhouse conditions, but are not so easy as the others. Species to look out for from this group include *L. flava*, which is yellow, *L. harpophylla* and *L. cinnabarina*, which are orange to red, and the spectacular, fiery red *L. milleri*.

Leptotes

Some orchids are best described as charming, and the three diminutive members of this genus clearly fit this description. They are related to laelias, and need careful cultivation in intermediate conditions, often thriving best when mounted on a piece of bark.

Leptotes unicolor has white or pale lilac flowers and *L. bicolor* is much the same, but with a deep purple streak down the centre of the lip.

Lycaste

Lycastes are amongst the easiest of orchids to grow, although special care is needed to produce the magnificent specimens often seen at shows and exhibitions. There are about twenty-five species from Mexico south to Peru and Bolivia, and most are deciduous, flowering in spring from the bare pseudobulbs at the same time as the new growths are starting.

Most are excellent subjects for a cool greenhouse, where their rather thin foliage needs good shade. When the leaves drop in autumn the plants need a dry and light position until the flowers appear in spring. During the short growing season they benefit from ample watering and feeding.

Lycaste cruenta and *L. aromatica* are similar yellow-flowered species with distinctive spicy perfumes. *Lycaste deppei* is similar in structure, but with white petals and green sepals spotted with reddish brown.

L. skinneri has large, pink flowers that can, in the best forms, be pure white or deep pink with a crimson-spotted lip. It was successfully grown as a house plant in Victorian times, when it thrived along with maidenhair ferns in the cool, shady damp of houses before central heating.

Many large-flowered hybrids have been produced, particularly using *L. skinneri* as a parent, and these should be grown in the same conditions as the species. Perhaps the best known in recent years is *L.* Auburn, many of which have won awards around the world.

Masdevallia

There are two hundred and fifty or so members of this fascinating genus of orchids. They range from Mexico south through tropical South America, but most are found in the cool cloud forests of the Andes. They have no pseudobulbs, so need constant moisture at the roots, and they particularly dislike summer heat and a dry atmosphere. All species are quite similar in vegetative appearance, but they produce a variety of different flowers. These are basically three partially fused sepals in the form of a trumpet, with much-reduced petals and lip.

This is a genus that has always attracted a dedicated group of enthusiastic specialists, for whom large showy hybrid orchids are really rather vulgar. I number some among my friends, so I hesitate to recommend species, daring only to suggest my own favourites.

Masdevallia veitchiana, with large red flowers, and *M. coccinea*, with slightly smaller magenta flowers, are musts, as is the delicate, white-flowered *M. tovarensis*. The pink flowers of *M. caudata* and the large orange and yellow flowers of *M. maculata* are also very worthy, as is the delicate *M. strobelii*.

In the past many hybrids were produced, and it is a testament to their vigour that many are still with us today. In recent years there has been an upsurge in interest in the genus, and new hybrids are now being produced. From the past I still like the large orange flowers of *M.* Kimballiana, and from the present the deep red of *M.* Prince Charming.

Maxillaria

Although this is a genus of over three hundred species distributed throughout the American tropics and subtropics, very few species are seen in cultivation. Most are epiphytes and need an intermediate greenhouse where their flowers, similar in shape to those of the genus *Lycaste*, are often produced in large numbers. Many species have a spicy scent, and for this feature alone many more should be grown.

The most spectacular member of the genus is *Maxillaria sanderiana*, which has large white flowers with a deep, purple-marked lip. *M. grandiflora* is often misidentified as this species, but, although similar, it lacks the spectacular lip.

The easiest to grow are the smaller-flowered types. Among these my particular favourites are the yellow-flowered species *M. lepidota* and *M. picta* and the deep-red-flowered *M. tenuifolia*.

Miltonia

This popular genus is traditionally divided into two distinct groups – the smaller-flowered Brazilian miltonias, which are easy to grow in intermediate conditions, and the Colombian miltonias, which are more demanding and require rather cooler conditions. This latter group is now, strictly speaking, placed in a new genus, *Miltoniopsis*. Its members produce the large, flat, scented flowers that give rise to the popular name of pansy orchids.

Among the twenty or so true miltonias the popular species are *Miltonia clowesii*, with a white and pink lip set against reddish-brown petals and sepals. Also seen are the pale yellow *M. flavescens* and *M. warscewiczii*, with its large, shiny red lip.

There are only five species of *Miltoniopsis*, but very many hybrids have been produced from them. Notable are the large-flowered species *Miltoniopsis roezlii* and *M. vexillaria*. Most of the popular hybrids trace their ancestry to just these two, and so could be thought of as all varieties of *Miltonia* Blueana, the primary hybrid between them. The attractive waterfall effect seen in some hybrids comes from *Miltoniopsis phalaenopsis*, a very attractive small-flowered species that has the reputation of being fiendishly difficult to grow.

Hybrid miltonias (strictly *Miltoniopsis* now) should be grown at the warm end of a cool greenhouse in humid shade. Some growers find them tricky, while others find them easy, even as house plants. I have at different times experienced them in both moods.

Neofinetia

There is but a single species in this genus – *Neofinetia falcata*, which comes from Japan, China, and Korea. A small monopodial epiphyte, it should be grown in humid shade in cool conditions. *N. falcata* is grown extensively as a house plant in the Far East. Particularly revered are variegated forms, and these are grown, and almost worshipped, for their foliage alone. The white flowers have a long, curved spur at the base of the lip.

Oncidium

This is a very large genus of over four hundred species native to the American tropics and subtropics. Many are very attractive, but only a few are commonly seen in cultivation. From so many I can select only a few favourites.

From Mexico comes the delightful cool-growing species *Oncidium ornithorhynchum*, with its profusion of tiny but highly scented pink flowers produced in autumn. Also from Mexico is the scented, yellow-flowered *O. tigrinum*.

From Central America, but this time warm growing, are two almost identical species, *O. papilio* and *O. kramerianum*. These have squat pseudobulbs and tough leaves mottled with maroon. In succession from the tip of a long spike are produced the large and spectacular orange and yellow flowers. They resemble the insect which gives rise to the common name of butterfly orchids, especially as they dance around in the slightest breeze on the end of the long, wiry spike. There is a hybrid between these two, *O.* Kalihi.

A number of very attractive species from Brazil have small yellow and brown flowers with proportionately large, bright yellow lips. Among these are *O. varicosum* and the slightly smaller *O. flexuosum*. A number of hybrids have been made using principally these two species, and these are even more spectacular and easier to grow.

Finally a selection of miniatures. *O. concolor*, as its name suggests, has flowers of an all-over bright yellow that are quite large for such a small plant. *O. cheirophorum* produces many more yellow flowers, but this time perfectly in proportion to the small plant.

Phragmipedium

These interesting slipper orchids are the American cousins of the paphiopedilums from the Far East; they number about fifteen species. They should be cultivated in shady conditions in an intermediate greenhouse. Being without pseudobulbs, they need constant moisture.

The large attractive flowers are produced in succession from an upright spike, and the extended petals of many species give them a bewhiskered oriental look. Popular examples are the pink-flowered *Phragmipedium schlimii* and the similar hybrid from it, *P.* Sedenii.

The dull green and pink flowers of *P. caudatum* have the longest petals in the genus. They continue to grow downward, after the flower has opened, until they reach the ground, and probably provide a route for pollinating insects. If the plant is grown in a pot it is possible to place it in such a position that the petals hang over the edge of the greenhouse staging. They then continue to extend to 2ft (60cm) or more, creating a spectacular effect.

Around the turn of the century a number of hybrids were made, and these are sometimes still available.

Pleione

These charming orchids originate in the cool mountains of northern India, Burma, south China, and Thailand, where they grow as epiphytes or lithophytes. They are unusual in that they are not only deciduous but also have annual pseudobulbs and roots.

The most common, and easiest of the dozen or so species, is *Pleione formosana*. There are a number of different shades of mauve available, as well as a pure white form, and an increasing range of excellent hybrids are being produced.

The bare pseudobulbs should be half-buried in well-drained compost, a number to a pot or pan, during late winter. The large flowers are produced with the new growths in spring, just as the new roots start. In autumn the leaves are shed from the new pseudobulbs, and the old pseudobulb shrivels away. They should be grown very cool, just frost-free, in shady conditions, and are often successful in a shady cold frame. Water and feed are required during the growing season, but they should be dry during the winter dormant period.

Pleurothallis

There may be as many as fifteen hundred species in this genus of mainly small, and to many people insignificant, orchids. They originate from tropical and subtropical America, with most from the montane forests of the Andes, and need cool or intermediate conditions with shade and humidity.

With such a large genus I hesitate to make recommendations. They are all fascinating little plants but none are spectacular or showy. These gems of the orchid world benefit from viewing through a hand lens, when their flower structure is revealed. A genus very much for the enthusiast.

Promenaea

Although there are fifteen or so members of this Brazilian genus, only two are commonly seen in cultivation. They are small epiphytic plants that freely produce large numbers of attractive flowers in summer. Shady intermediate conditions suit them best.

Promenaea xanthina has large, lemon-yellow flowers, while its relative, *P. stapelioides*, has green flowers with heavy spotting of dark purple and an almost black lip.

A number of fine hybrids has been produced in recent years, and there is also an interesting intergeneric hybrid with *Zygopetalum* known as *Propetalum* Mathina. This has the characteristic upright spike of several flowers from the *Zygopetalum*, combined with the yellow colour from *P. xanthina*.

Restrepia

There are thirty or so species distributed from Mexico south to Argentina. They are closely related to the genus *Pleurothallis*, but although also miniatures they are somewhat more showy. They should be cultivated in cool or intermediate conditions, with plenty of shade and humidity, and as they have no pseudobulbs they need constant moisture.

The freely produced flowers defy description, resembling a rather strange insect. *Restrepia antennifera* is the most commonly seen, but there are several other quite similar species around. They are fascinating little orchids, and quite easy to grow.

Rhynchostylis

Although there are only four members of this monopodial genus, they are all popular and commonly seen in cultivation. Their home is the tropical forests of southeast Asia, and they need warm and moist conditions to grow well.

The thick, waxy, and highly fragrant flowers are produced in pendent cylindrical racemes, which give them their common name of foxtail orchids. Most have white or pink flowers, some with the addition of mauve or magenta spotting.

Rhynchostylis retusa and *R. gigantea* are commonly available, and either can be recommended for inclusion in a warm-house collection.

Many hybrids with other related genera including *Vanda* have been produced in the Far East. These are little known as yet, but deserve to be grown more widely.

Rossioglossum

The five or so species in this Central American genus were formerly included in the genus *Odontoglossum*, and are better known under that name. They are easy plants for the cool greenhouse, where they benefit from a dry, cool, and light winter rest.

The best known, and indeed one of the most popular of all tropical orchids, is *Rossioglossum grande*, the clown orchid. It is easy to grow, and is often seen as a house plant. The large, spectacular, chocolate and yellow flowers are produced in autumn and last for several weeks, and no collection should be without this old favourite.

Sophronitis

There is nothing quite so strikingly red as a well-grown sophronitis in full bloom. There are seven members of this genus of miniature Brazilian orchids, and one, *Sophronitis coccinea*, has been popular ever since its first introduction in 1836.

These orchids are similar to miniature cattleyas, producing flowers of a size out of all proportion to the plant. They need cool or intermediate shady conditions, and should be constantly moist. They are often successful in a shallow pan or mounted on a piece of bark.

Stanhopea

There are about twenty-five species in this genus, widely distributed throughout the American tropics. They are unusual epiphytes in that the flower spike, which is produced from the base of the pseudobulb, grows vertically downward through the compost, producing its flowers beneath the plant. This present no difficulty in the wild, but clearly it must be grown in a basket in cultivation.

Stanhopeas are easy plants to grow, suspended from the roof in a cool or intermediate greenhouse. Although the flowers last for only a few days they are large and fascinating structures and they have the most overpowering perfume. *Stanhopea wardii*, with pale, yellow-spotted flowers, and *S. tigrina*, with large, cream flowers heavily blotched with dark maroon, are particular favourites. No orchid collection should be without one, even if only for the reaction of visitors to their bizarre flowers.

Trichopilia

About thirty species are found in the tropics of Central and South America, where they grow as forest epiphytes. In cultivation an intermediate greenhouse is ideal, with good shade and plenty of moisture during the growing season. The flowers are produced horizontally on short stems from the base of the pseudobulbs.

Trichopilia tortilis, with its curiously twisted petals and sepals is perhaps the best known. Also popular is the pink flowered *T. suavis*, but nothing is quite so spectacular as a good, dark red form of *T. marginata* in full bloom. Unfortunately this species is rarely seen.

Vanda

There are about forty species in this variable genus, distributed throughout tropical Asia, southeast Asia, Indo-China, and as far as Australia. They are monopodial plants without pseudobulbs, and with one or two exceptions require warm greenhouse conditions. The many hybrids are grown as cut flowers in southeast Asia, particularly in Singapore and Thailand, for export around the world.

The most popular species is *Vanda coerulea*, which comes from the hills of northern India and Burma and is therefore somewhat cooler growing. It is a variable species, with the best examples clear blue – a colour rare in orchids.

More common are the many hybrids from the Philippine species *V. sanderiana* (now often known as *Euanthe sanderiana*), with their characteristic large, round, flat flowers in colours from purple and mauve through red to orange and yellow, with net-veined patterns particularly on the lower sepals. If there is room for just one, then the magnificent deep blue hybrid *V. Rothschildiana*, a cross between *V. coerulea* and *V. sanderiana* is the one to grow, but beware – it is also very variable.

Vandas have been hybridized with many other genera. This breeding has been largely inspired by the Far Eastern cut-flower trade, but many make fine plants for collectors. Notable among the many are the compact hybrids between *Vanda* and *Ascocentrum*, which makes the hybrid genus *Ascocenda*.

Zygopetalum

There appear to be something between twenty and forty members of this genus, depending on which expert you follow. They are epiphytes from tropical South America, and should be grown in good shade in an intermediate greenhouse. Only two or three species are likely to be seen in cultivation, and they are particularly valued for their blue colour and their delicate perfume, both welcome in the depth of winter.

Zygopetalum crinitum and *Z. intermedium* are quite similar and both are easy plants to grow, but I would recommend the hybrids. The best of these have been micropropagated and offer superb blue lips and larger, fuller flowers than the species.

HYBRID ORCHIDS

The most popular orchids for the amateur enthusiast come from those groups where most hybrids have been produced. These are not mutually exclusive, but most growers end up specializing in one or perhaps two of these areas, often with a few favourite species from other genera. A brief look at these groups follows.

Cattleyas

Cattleyas are for many people the 'Queen of Orchids'. They are the large, frilled, and richly coloured flowers, usually purple, that we see on chocolate boxes and greetings cards.

There are between thirty and fifty different species in this New World genus, depending on how we regard the many varieties, particularly the varieties of *Cattleya labiata*. Horticulturally the genus is usually divided into two main groups, with a few odds and ends that do not quite conform.

The first section, known as the 'labiate' or 'unifoliate' cattleyas, comprises *C. labiata* and its many varieties and variants, together with a few related species. These species come from Central and northern South America and have spindle-shaped or club-shaped pseudobulbs with a solitary leaf. The large, frilly, and rather delicate flowers are usually produced singly or in pairs from the apex of the pseudobulbs. These, or their hybrids, are the orchids on the chocolate boxes and are often used for large corsages.

C. labiata itself is a variable species from eastern Brazil. The best forms have lilac and purple flowers, up to 6in (15cm) across, with a deep purple, yellow-throated lip. *C. warscewiczii* has even larger flowers of rose pink with a carmine and yellow lip, and *C. trianae* is similar, but with pale, almost white, petals and sepals. Others in this group include *C. gaskelliana*, *C. eldorado*, and *C. mendelii*.

For many enthusiasts the gem of this section is *C.*

dowiana. This magnificent species comes from Costa Rica and Colombia, and is now quite rare in the wild. The large flowers are a beautiful, delicate yellow with a rich, velvety, crimson-purple lip. The centre of the lip has a number of radiating golden yellow veins which in the variety *aurea* are richer and intricately branching. This species has been used extensively in breeding for its magnificently marked lip and for its unusual yellow colour.

The second and larger section of the genus consists of plants with rather thinner, cane-like pseudobulbs, each with two or more leaves. These 'bifoliate' cattleyas produce smaller but rather more numerous flowers of heavier texture.

C. bowringiana, with up to twenty purple 3in (7.5cm) flowers, and the similar *C. skinneri*, are perhaps the best known. *C. aurantiaca* produces drooping clusters of orange flowers in summer, and *C. bicolor* has green to brown flowers with a contrasting bright pink lip. Other recommendations in this section are *C. amethystoglossa*, white with pink spotting, *C. granulosa* and *C. leopoldii*.

The first registered hybrid, *Cattleya* Dominiana, flowered in 1859 and since then many fine hybrids have been made. *Cattleya* Bow Bells, a magnificent large white, remains a favourite, but there are so many. In recent years more attention has been paid to the smaller bifoliate species, and many modern hybrids with heavy texture include blood from this group.

In 1863 the first intergeneric hybrid, *Laeliocattleya* Exoniensis, a cross between a *Cattleya* and a *Laelia*, flowered at the famous nursery of Veitch. Laelias are used to introduce yellow and orange, to increase the number and improve the texture of flowers, and to introduce hybrid vigour. Laeliocattleyas are generally very easy to grow.

Soon other genera were hybridized with cattleyas. *Brassavola digbyana* is rather difficult to grow, but has a huge fringed lip. It was bred with cattleyas and laelias to introduce this lip, and produced spectacular hybrids in several new genera – *Brassocattleya*, *Brassolaelia*, and *Brassolaeliocattleya*.

The tiny species *Sophronitis coccinea* introduced deep scarlet and red, and small stature, to a further set of hybrids – *Sophrocattleya*, *Sophrolaeliocattleya*, and *Potinara* (involving the four genera *Sophronitis*, *Laelia*, *Cattleya*, and *Brassavola*). In recent years *Epidendrum* has been used to create yet another group, and further complex hybrids.

Most of the species and all of the hybrids can be grown together in an intermediate greenhouse, indeed in the days when collections were cultivated in a number of greenhouses, this house was often referred to as the cattleya house. Many are suitable for windowsill culture, particularly those of smaller stature.

Cattleyas like a pleasant, light, evenly warm, and humid environment, and dislike large changes in temperature. A winter night minimum of 55°F (13°C) should be maintained, with a rise during the day and a rise both day and night during the summer of 5–10°F (2–5°C). Light to medium shading is needed in late spring and summer, but winter-flowering plants benefit from a few weeks light and dryish rest at the end of the growing season. Humidity should be maintained throughout the year but should not be excessive. It should follow the temperature – highest when the temperature is highest.

Cattleyas should be potted in an open, well-drained compost so that they can be heavily watered during the growing season without fear of soggy conditions.

Cymbidiums

Cymbidiums are perhaps the most popular of all groups with amateur growers. They are easy to grow, requiring only cool conditions, and the large abundant flowers, available in a wide range of colours, last for many weeks. They are also the most popular of orchids for commercial cut-flower production outside the tropics.

There are about fifty species found from the northern hills of India through southeast Asia to China, Japan, and Australia. They grow in cool mountain forest areas, mostly as epiphytes, but with some terrestrials. Most have characteristic egg-shaped pseudobulbs with a number of long, narrow, leathery leaves. The peak of the flowering season is early spring, with some hybrids especially bred to produce flowers in autumn and winter.

Most cymbidium growers do not bother with species, preferring a mixed collection of hybrids, but there are a few species worthy of inclusion. *Cymbidium lowianum* from India and Burma produces long, arching spikes of yellow-green flowers in late spring. The red marking on the lip of this species is inherited and is seen in many modern hybrids. Also from India is *C. hookerianum*, which has flowers of the most intense green. As with all green cymbidiums it should be shaded from the sun to prevent the flowers fading to yellow.

C. tracyanum from Burma flowers in autumn, producing sprays of large, scented, yellow flowers, heavily striped and spotted with reddish brown. Other species include the beautifully scented pink *C. parishii*, and two favourite miniatures – *C. devonianum* with its pendulous sprays of green and purple flowers and the late-spring-flowering yellow species *C. tigrinum*.

Most of the many thousands of registered hybrids have been produced from just a few large-flowered species. These standard cymbidiums are generally quite large plants with spikes of a dozen or more flowers, each 4–5in (10–12cm) wide, in colours from red through pink to orange, yellow, green, and white, usually with lips blotched or spotted with red. Some are an overall even colour, without the red markings on the lip, and many of these have been produced in Australia, where they are very popular. The heavy-textured flowers of modern standard cymbidiums last for many weeks either on the plant or cut in water.

Standard cymbidiums are bred for the commercial cut-flower industry, and can be rather large plants for an amateur greenhouse. In more recent times there has been considerable interest in breeding miniature cymbidiums, although the distinction is now blurred by an increasing number of intermediate sizes.

Miniature cymbidiums are produced by crossing the standard hybrids with one of the miniature species. *C. pumilum* has been used for many years, producing a race of plants with upright, multiflowered spikes. Further hybridizing has enlarged the individual flowers, but in some cases also the foliage. The unfortunate result has been standard-sized plants with small flowers. Attractive miniatures with pendulous spikes have been produced from *C. devonianum*. These have well-shaped flowers, often with a distinctive dark red lip, and fortunately inherit shorter, wider foliage from the species parent. Yet another group of miniatures has been bred from *C. tigrinum*, a species used for its small stature and particularly squat foliage. Hybrids tend to have relatively large but fewer flowers, produced in late spring or early summer.

Cymbidiums are plants for the cool greenhouse, where a winter night minimum of 50°F (10°C) can be maintained. An occasional drop below this will do no harm, especially as the plants are normally kept on the dry side during the winter months. A few degrees warmer during the day is desirable, as is a warmer spring and summer growing season. They need enough shade to prevent scorching, especially of the new foliage in spring, but a drop in temperature at night in summer and a light, cool, and airy autumn are essential for flowering. Spring and summer are the months of maximum growth, when they should have high humidity and be watered and fed frequently.

Cymbidiums should be re-potted in spring in an open, free-draining compost, either bark- or peat-based, every two or three years, at which time the plants may be divided. In normal circumstances it is best to try to grow good large plants as they look so spectacular in full flower. However, if the plant has developed a bare centre it will need dividing into pieces each of not less than three green pseudobulbs with foliage.

Cymbidiums, particularly miniatures, are often sold as house plants, but they are far from ideal for this purpose. Some orchids can be successful indoors, but cymbidiums must have good light, good humidity, and cool nights in summer and good light and cool conditions in winter, to grow and flower. This does not fit very well with our central heating, which we do tend to use in winter!

Odontoglossums

These diverse, beautiful, winter-flowering species and hybrids were the firm favourites of amateurs of the past, long before cymbidiums came along. They remain popular in those temperate areas of the world where they can be grown, and an ever-expanding list of intergeneric hybrids is increasing their tolerance of varied conditions. For horticultural purposes a number of related genera and their hybrids are included in the general term odontoglossums. The flowers are among the most showy in the orchid family, and generally last for many weeks, either on the plant or as cut flowers in water.

The genus *Odontoglossum* consists of a hundred or more usually epiphytic species confined mainly to the mountains of tropical and subtropical Central and South America. They are pseudobulbous plants, most of which produce attractive flowers in winter at the beginning or the end of a rest period. In the wild this would be the drier, brighter season.

The finest of the genus, if not of the whole orchid family, must be *Odontoglossum crispum*. Frederick Boyle, the Victorian writer, never one to understate his case, described it as the most supremely beautiful creation in the whole of nature. For thirty years or so at the end of the last century hundreds of thousands, if not millions, were stripped from the Andes of Colombia and sold in Europe.

Fine, large, pure white forms, and some attractively marked varieties, changed hands for thousands of pounds in the frenzy to own these gems. Most soon died, and all that now remains is a collection of paintings and a host of hybrids.

O. crispum and its relative *O. pescatorei* are not easy to grow, but they are the basis for many thousands of far easier hybrids. Stick with the hybrids is my advice, but if you must try these species then make sure you are purchasing nursery-raised plants. Previous generations of orchid enthusiasts reduced these species to near extinction; we must not be guilty of contributing to its completion.

O. bictoniense was the first of the genus to be introduced into cultivation, and remains a firm favourite. It is easy to grow and flower, producing upright spikes of many small, pink-lipped, brown flowers. *O. pulchellum*, *O. rossii*, and *O. cervantesii* are all compact, desirable plants.

Almost all the species are attractive, and it is difficult to choose recommendations, but a particular personal favourite is *O. harryanum*, with its large lip marked with purple. For many years it was rarely seen, but it has recently been raised from seed from a fine clone, and should remain readily available.

The early hybrids were based on the best forms of *O. crispum*, crossed and back-crossed with related species, and many times with further crispums. With so much blood from one source it is not surprising that they were all similar in shape and size to *O. crispum* itself, but in a wider range of colours, and were equally tricky to grow well. There are fewer straight *Odontoglossum* hybrids being produced today, as they have been replaced by easier and more adaptable intergenerics.

Odontoglossums hybridize readily with each other, and with related genera. The first of these to be involved was the small, red-flowered genus *Cochlioda*, from which was produced *Odontioda*. These were originally produced to improve the red hybrids, but further breeding has given us odontiodas in a wide range of colours. Miltonias were used to give *Odontonia*, with large flowers and large lips. *Vuylstekeara* is the result of a combination of these three genera.

More recently the introduction of *Oncidium* has produced hybrids more tolerant of warmth. There are many attractive, predominantly yellow-flowered members of the genus *Odontocidium* (*Odontoglossum* × *Oncidium*), and an increasing number of variously coloured *Wilsonara* (*Odontoglossum*, *Oncidium*, and *Cochlioda*) hybrids. Further breeding with other related genera has produced many interesting intergeneric hybrids, and this will certainly continue in the future.

Odontoglossums and their allies are ideal subjects for a cool greenhouse. Most species, and most hybrids, are easy to grow and flower. Unfortunately, the favourites, such as *O. crispum* and the hybrids that are mostly of this species, are intolerant of less than ideal conditions.

To grow odontoglossums well requires a minimum winter night temperature of 50°F (10°C), with a day-time rise of a few degrees and similar rise both day and night in summer. They require good shade from direct sun, with high humidity, particularly when the temperature rises. They grow in the wild at altitude, and the problem is that it is difficult to reproduce these fresh, cool, and humid conditions at sea level. They do not like high temperatures, and to keep them cool in summer we must resort to ventilation. This lets out the humidity, but they also dislike dry air. In summer we must therefore mainly use external shading to prevent the temperature rising too high, and carefully juggle the ventilation and moisture. In winter they dislike cold and damp together, but must not be totally dry. As the temperature falls the relative humidity naturally rises, so we must be very careful to water and damp down in the morning when the temperature is rising. Basically what they will not tolerate is a combination of low temperatures with high humidity or high temperatures and low humidity.

The intergeneric hybrids are progressively easier as their parentage moves away from the influence of *O. crispum*. Odontiodas are a little easier than pure odontoglossums. Odontonias and vuylstekearas have miltonia blood in their make up and so benefit from a little more warmth. Odontocidiums and wilsonaras have oncidium blood and require a little more warmth and light. They are more tolerant of higher summer temperatures, and, if given sufficient light, are often grown successfully as house plants.

Paphiopedilums

These are the popular lady's slipper orchids that were formerly referred to as *Cypripedium*. They usually grow as terrestrials and have no pseudobulbs, the plants consisting of tufts of often leathery leaves. The flowers are produced singly, or sometimes on a multiflowered stem, from the centre of these tufted growths. Literally thousands of hybrids have been produced, and many have large and showy flowers that last for weeks and sometimes months.

There are about sixty species distributed throughout southeast Asia from northern India through Burma, China, and Indonesia to the Philippines. With such a wide distribution it is not surprising that they have different cultural requirements.

A number of popular species are found in northern India, where they grow at altitude in cool valleys. *Paphiopedilum fairrieanum*, with attractive purple-veined flowers, is one of the best known. From the same climate comes the green and brown species *P. insigne*, which at one time was grown in vast quantities for the cut-flower trade, *P. spicerianum*, with green, white, and pink flowers, and *P. hirsutissimum*, with shiny mauve patches on its twisted petals. *P. venustum* has multi-coloured flowers and attractive mottled foliage.

Burma and Thailand are the homes of a number of related species of dwarf stature with mottled leaves and large, round, spotted flowers. *P. bellatulum* has white flowers with maroon spotting, *P. godefroyae* has similar cream-to-yellow flowers, and *P. niveum* has clear white flowers with a little light speckling. Vietnam was the home of the beautiful, fragrant, pink *P. delenatii*. This favourite species may well be extinct in the wild, and its survival in cultivation is entirely due to the dedicated work of one nursery in France, where it has been raised many times from seed.

In the last few years a number of new species have been introduced from the remote regions of western China. These are fascinating species with large, pouch-shaped, highly coloured lips, quite unlike most other members of the genus, but showing some similarities with *P. delenatii*. They have not been in cultivation long enough for there to be any nursery-raised stock yet, despite what it might say on the export permits issued in the Far East, so my advice is to wait until there is.

Another group of warm-growing species with characteristic mottled foliage also continues to be popular. *P. curtisii*, *P. callosum*, *P. purpuratum*, and *P. barbatum* all produce single flowers on long stems in various colour combinations of green and purple, each with a dominant striped dorsal sepal.

Members of the final group are all large, warm-growing plants with plain green foliage and several flowers on each spike. *P. parishii* often grows as an epiphyte with a pendent spike of green and purple flowers. *P. chamberlainianum* and *P. glaucophyllum* produce a succession of pink, pouched flowers from an extending spike. Perhaps the finest of all are the upright-growing species *P. philippinense*, with yellow flowers, and the spectacular *P. rothschildianum*, with purple-striped flowers 12in (30cm) or more from petal tip to petal tip.

For many years the production of hybrids was dominated by the requirements of the cut-flower trade, which needed large, round, flat, waxy flowers on good stems that would last quite literally for months. There are enthusiasts who collect these standard paphiopedilums, and they continue to gain awards, but, like standard cymbidiums, they have probably reached their ultimate development.

These standard hybrids were produced using a number of different species. *P. insigne*, *P. villosum*, and *P. spicerianum* were used in the early days. *P. bellatulum* and its relatives added their round shape, but unfortunately sometimes also their short flower stem. Most colours are available, although good reds and clear pinks are still somewhat elusive.

The clear green and white flowers of *P.* Maudiae produced in 1900 by crossing albino forms of the species *P. lawrenceanum* and *P. callosum*, remain popular, as do other similar hybrids produced by further breeding.

In recent years there has been a resurgence of interest in primary hybrids, some as remakes of old hybrids and some entirely new. Particularly popular are the large multiflowered hybrids from *P. rothschildianum* and other similar species. Now that the spectacular *P. sanderianum* has been re-discovered, and the new species from China are established in breeding programmes, we can look forward to an entirely new set of interesting hybrids in the not-too-distant future.

Most of the hybrids are grown in intermediate conditions, but a number of the Indian species are perfectly happy in a cool greenhouse. Some of the mottled-leaved species, and the Maudiae-type hybrids, together with the large species such as *P. rothschildianum*, prefer a warm greenhouse.

Paphiopedilums have no water-storage organs, so they should be kept constantly moist at the roots. The compost should be sufficiently open and well drained so that this constantly moist condition does not become soggy.

Humidity should be fairly high, especially when the temperature is high, and good shade should be provided in spring and summer.

Many paphiopedilums can be grown as house plants. Select the cool-growing Indian species for a cool room and any of the standard hybrids for the warmer parts of the house. Good light without direct sun is needed, together with some means of providing local humidity. They are ideal subjects for a growing case.

Phalaenopsis

These orchids, commonly called moth orchids, are increasing in popularity with amateur growers. Although they require warm conditions, they produce an abundance of mainly white, pink, and yellow flowers all year round, and well-grown mature hybrids can be permanently in flower. Certainly a good collection should have 80 per cent of the plants in bloom at any one time.

There are forty-six or so species distributed throughout southeast Asia from India through Indonesia to northern Australia, with the greatest concentration in the Philippines. Almost all are tropical epiphytes with a plant structure unlikely to be confused with any other genus.

They are monopodial plants without pseudobulbs. They have short, thick, central stems from which grow a number of broad, usually drooping, leathery leaves. The flower spikes are produced from between these leaves, and in many species the spike bears many large attractive flowers that last for many weeks. Most growers prefer the many attractive hybrids, but among the species the white-flowered *Phalaenopsis amabilis*, *P. aphrodite*, and *P. stuartiana* remain popular. *P. stuartiana* has interestingly spotted flowers, and the added attraction of mottled foliage.

Also with mottled foliage is *P. schilleriana*, which produces long spikes with as many as three hundred pink flowers. Several smaller-flowered species are also seen in collections, including *P. lueddemanniana*, a variable yellowish spotted species from the Philippines, *P. equestris*, with delicate pink flowers, and *P. mariae*, with maroon spotted flowers on short spikes.

Finally, a very popular species from Borneo and Malaya is *P. violacea*. Although this species has only a few flowers at a time they have the most delightful perfume.

Still the most popular of the hybrids are the large whites, produced from many generations of selective breeding. The best have perfectly round, flat flowers over 5in (12.5cm) across, borne on long spikes. Most cut and last very well; they are popular for wedding bouquets.

Most pink hybrids are not quite so enormous, but in all other respects are similar. They are available in shades from pale pink through to deep pink, almost magenta. Breeding with *Doritis* has produced *Doritaenopsis*, with even richer-coloured, if somewhat smaller, pink flowers. Some pink hybrids from *P. violacea* retain the perfume of the species.

The selective use of the species *P. equestris* and *P. lindenii* has produced a race of white hybrids with deep red lips, and others with pink candy stripes on the petals and sepals. More recently several smaller-flowered species have been used to produce yellow flowers, the best of which are very attractive and do not fade.

As well as *Doritaenopsis*, a number of other interesting intergeneric hybrids are being produced. *Phalaenopsis* sometimes breed with *Vanda* to produce *Vandaenopsis*, and this may eventually be the route to blue flowers, but one group very well worth looking out for is the delightful multiflowered *Renanthopsis* hybrids, which result from a cross between *Phalaenopsis* and *Renanthera*.

Phalaenopsis are easy plants to grow and flower, but they must have warmth. An absolute minimum of 60°F (16°C) at night must be maintained, and they are far better if the minimum is maintained a few degrees above this. They require a rise in temperature during the day, and a further rise in summer. Maintaining a greenhouse at these temperatures is certainly expensive, but fortunately *Phalaenopsis* must have good shade, so lining the greenhouse to conserve heat is perfectly acceptable.

Apart from warmth and shade, *Phalaenopsis* must have high humidity. They do not have pseudobulbs and grow all year round, so they must be constantly moist. They are relatively fast-growing plants, and need regular feeding. As they are epiphytes their roots need air, so they should be potted in a coarse, open compost.

Many growers are successful with *Phalaenopsis* indoors. Unlike many plants they relish the even warmth of modern centrally heated homes, and are happy in lower light levels than most orchids. The only problem is humidity, particularly around the roots, but if this can be overcome with a growing case, or by the use of wet gravel trays or other ingenious means, then they will thrive. If you are successful with African violets (*Saintpaulia*), then you will succeed with *Phalaenopsis*.

BIBLIOGRAPHY

Arditti, J., *Orchid Biology: Reviews and Perspectives*, Cornell University Press, New York and London, 1977

Bechtel, H., Cribb, P., & Launert, E., *The Manual of Cultivated Orchid Species*, Blandford, Dorset, 1981

Darwin, C., *The Various Contrivances by which Orchids are Fertilized by Insects*, John Murray, London, 1862

Dressler, R. L. *The Orchids: Natural History and Classification*, Harvard University Press, Cambridge, Mass., and London, 1981

Hawkes, A.D., *Encyclopaedia of Cultivated Orchids*, Faber & Faber, London, 1965

Kramer, J., *Growing Orchids at your Windows*, D. van Nostrand, New York, 1963

Noble, M., *You Can Grow Orchids*, M. Noble, Florida, 1964

Northen, R. T., *Home Orchid Growing*, Van Nostrand Reinhold, New York, 1970

Rittershausen, P.R.C., *Successful Orchid Culture*, Collingridge, London, 1953

Rittershausen, B. and Rittershausen, W., *Popular Orchids*, Stockwell, Devon, 1970

Sander, D. F., *Orchids and their Cultivation*, Blandford, London, 1962

Swinson, A., *Frederick Sander: The Orchid King*, Hodder & Stoughton, London, 1970

Williams, B. S., *Orchid Growers' Manual*, Wheldon & Wesley, Herts, 1894

Withner, C. L., *The Orchids: A Scientific Survey*, The Ronald Press, New York, 1959

Withner, C. L., *The Orchids: Scientific Studies*, Wiley, New York and London, 1974

Veitch, J. & Sons, *Manual of Orchidaceous Plants*, H. M. Pollett, London, 1887

JOURNALS

American Orchid Society Bulletin, American Orchid Society, 6000 South Olive Avenue, West Palm Beach, Florida 33405, USA

Australian Orchid Review, The Australian Orchid Council, 14 McGill Street, Sydney, Australia, 2049

The Canadian Orchid Journal, The Canadian Orchid Journal Society Inc., P.O. Box 9472, Station B, St. John's, Newfoundland, Canada, A1A 2Y4

Die Orchidee, Deutsche Orchideen-Gesellschaft, Frankfurt, West Germany

Orchids in New Zealand, The New Zealand Orchid Society, Wellington, New Zealand

The Orchid Advocate, Cymbidium Society of America Inc., 931 Hermes Avenue, Leucadia, California 92024, USA

The Orchid Digest, The Orchid Digest Corporation, 1801 North C Street, Oxnard, California 93030, USA

The Orchid Review, The Orchid Review Ltd, New Gate Farm, Scotchey Lane, Stour Provost, Gillingham, Dorset, SP8 5LT, England

The South African Orchid Journal, The South African Orchid Council, P.O. Box 2678, Johannesburg 2000, South Africa

NURSERIES

United Kingdom

Burnham Nurseries, Forches Cross, Newton Abbot, Devon, TQ12 6PZ

Greenaway Orchids, Rookery Farm, Puxton, Weston-super-Mare, Avon, BS24 6TL

Mansell & Hatcher Ltd, Cragg Wood Nurseries, Rawdon, Leeds, LS19 6LQ

McBean's Orchids Ltd, Cooksbridge, Lewes, East Sussex, BN8 4PR

Ratcliffes Orchids Ltd, Owlesbury, Winchester, Hampshire, SO21 1LR

David Stead Orchids Ltd, Langley Farm, Westgate Lane, Lofthouse, Wakefield, West Yorkshire, WF3 3PA

Thatched Lodge Orchids, 92 Burys Bank Road, Greenham Common North, Newbury, Berkshire, RG15 8DD

Wyld Court Orchids, Hampstead Norreys, Newbury, Berkshire, RG16 0TN

United States of America

Aloha Orchids, P.O. Box 433, Makawao, Hawaii 96768

Cloud Forest Orchids, P.O. Box 370, Honokaa, Hawaii 96727

Fennell Orchid Company, 26715 S.W. 157 Avenue, Homestead, Florida 33031

Fordyce Orchids, 1330 Isabel Avenue, Livermore, California 94550

J. & L. Orchids, 20 Sherwood Road, Easton, Connecticut 06612

Jones & Scully, 18955 S.W. 168th Street, Miami, Florida 33187

Orchid Art, 1433 Kew Avenue, Hewlett, NY 11557

Orchids by Hausermann, 2N 134 Addison Road, Villa Park, IL 60181

R. F. Orchids, 28100 SW 182nd Avenue, Homestead, FL 33030

Rod McLellan Co., 1450 El Camino Real, South San Francisco, California 94080

Santa Barbara Orchid Estate, 1250 Orchid Drive, Santa Barbara, California 93111

Stewart Orchids, 3376 Foothill Road, Carpinteria, California 93013

Zuma Canyon Orchids, 5949 Bonsall Drive, Malibu, California 90265

Others

ABC Orchid Corporation, P.O. Box 105–075, Taipei, Taiwan, Republic of China

Adelaide Orchids, Box 1, O'Halloran Hill, S.A. 5158, Australia

Duckitt Nurseries, Darling, Cape Town, South Africa

Geyserland Orchids, P.O. Box 162, Rotorua, New Zealand

Kabukiran Orchids, 81 Maginoo Street, Quezon City 1100, Philippines

Katsuura Shoyoen Orchid Co., 4-6-20 Kitakasugaoka, Ibaraki, Osaka 567, Japan

Kultana Orchids, 39/6 Soi Wat Nawong, Song Prabha Road, Bangkok 10210, Thailand

Lemforder Orchideen, 2844 Lemforder, Am Rauhen Berge 3, West Germany

Nindethana Orchids, Box 94, Mitcham, Victoria 3132, Australia

Norm Porter Orchids, 23 Parata Street, Waikanae, New Zealand

Orchideen Wubben, Tolakkerweg 162–3739, JT Holl, Rading, Holland

Orquideario Catarinense, P.O. Box 1, 89280 Corupta, Santa Catarina, Brazil

Vacherot & Lecoufle, La Tuilerie, 30 Rue de Valenton, 94470 Boissey-Saint-Leger, France

Valley Orchids, Box 220, Morphett Vale, S.A. 5162, Australia

Wichmann Orchideen, P.O. Box 111, Tannholtzweg 1–3, 3100 Celle, West Germany

COLLECTIONS TO VISIT

United Kingdom

The Royal Botanic Gardens, Kew, Richmond, Surrey
The Royal Horticultural Society Gardens, Wisley, Surrey
Oxford University Botanic Garden, High Street, Oxford
The Royal Botanic Garden, Edinburgh, Scotland
The Glasgow Botanic Gardens, Glasgow, Scotland
The Eric Young Orchid Foundation, Victoria Village,
    Trinity, Jersey, Channel Islands

United States of America

The Marie Selby Botanical Gardens, 811 South Palm
    Avenue, Sarasota, Florida 34236
University of California Botanical Garden, Centennial
Drive, Berkeley, California 94720
Brooklyn Botanic Garden, 1000 Washington Avenue,
    Brooklyn, New York 11225
Foster Botanical Garden, Honolulu, Hawaii
Missouri Botanical Garden, St Louis, Missouri
New York Botanical Garden, Southern Boulevard,
    Bronx, New York

Others

Royal Botanic Gardens, Sydney, Australia
Jardim Botanico de Rio de Janeiro, Rio de Janeiro,
    Brazil
Jardim Botanico de São Paulo, São Paulo, Brazil
Jardin Botanique de Montreal, Montreal, Canada
University Botanic Garden, Copenhagen, Denmark
National Botanic Gardens, Dublin, Eire
Jardin des Plantes, Paris, France
Palmengarten, Frankfurt, West Germany
University Botanic Garden, Leiden, Holland
Hortus Bogoriense, Kebun Raya, Bogor, Java, Indonesia
Botanic Gardens, Penang, Malaysia
Christchurch Botanic Gardens, Christchurch, New
    Zealand
Singapore Botanic Gardens, Cluny Road, Singapore
Komarov Botanical Institute Garden, Leningrad, USSR

SOCIETIES

United Kingdom

The British Orchid Council, 20 Newbury Drive,
    Davyhulme, Manchester, M31 2FA
The Orchid Society of Great Britain, 28 Felday Road,
    Lewisham, London SE13

United States of America

American Orchid Society, 6000 South Olive Avenue,
    West Palm Beach, Florida 33405
The Cymbidium Society of America, 6881 Wheeler
    Avenue, Westminster, California 92683

INDEX

Page numbers in *italics* refer to captions to the colour plates.